RESEARCH AND THE
COMPLEX CAUSALITY OF THE
SCHIZOPHRENIAS

Research and the Complex Causality of the Schizophrenias

Formulated by the
Committee on Research

Group for the Advancement of Psychiatry

BRUNNER/MAZEL *Publishers* • New York

Library of Congress Cataloging in Publication Data

Main entry under title.

Research and the complex causality of the schizophrenias.

  Bibliography: p.
  Includes index.
  1. Schizophrenia—Etiology—Research. I. Group for
the Advancement of Psychiatry. Committee on Research.
[DNLM: 1. Research—methods. 2. Schizophrenia—etiology.
WM 203 R432]
RC514.R47 1984   616.89'82   84-9535
ISBN 0-87630-373-4

Copyright © 1984 by the Group for the Advancement of Psychiatry

Published by
BRUNNER/MAZEL, INC.
19 Union Square West
New York, New York 10003

MANUFACTURED IN THE UNITED STATES OF AMERICA

This report is dedicated to the memory of Alfred H. Stanton, M.D., who contributed to the development of this report until his death in April, 1983. We hope that his dedication both to the ideals of GAP and to high standards of research is reflected in this report.

STATEMENT OF PURPOSE

THE GROUP FOR THE ADVANCEMENT OF PSYCHIATRY has a membership of approximately 300 psychiatrists, most of whom are organized in the form of a number of working committees. These committees direct their efforts toward the study of various aspects of psychiatry and the application of this knowledge to the fields of mental health and human relations.

Collaboration with specialists in other disciplines has been and is one of GAP's working principles. Since the formation of GAP in 1946 its members have worked closely with such other specialists as anthropologists, biologists, economists, statisticians, educators, lawyers, nurses, psychologists, sociologists, social workers, and experts in mass communication, philosophy, and semantics. GAP envisages a continuing program of work according to the following aims:

1. To collect and appraise significant data in the fields of psychiatry, mental health, and human relations
2. To reevaluate old concepts and to develop and test new ones
3. To apply the knowledge thus obtained for the promotion of mental health and good human relations

GAP is an independent group, and its reports represent the composite findings and opinions of its members only, guided by its many consultants.

RESEARCH AND THE COMPLEX CAUSALITY OF THE SCHIZOPHRENIAS was formulated by the Committee on Research. The members of this committee are listed on the next page. The following pages list the members of the other GAP committees, as well as additional membership categories and current and past officers of GAP.

Committee on Research
Group for the Advancement of Psychiatry
Jerry M. Lewis, M.D., Chairman

John E. Adams, M.D.
Robert Cancro, M.D.
Stanley H. Eldred, M.D.
John G. Gunderson, M.D.
Morris A. Lipton, M.D.
John G. Looney, M.D.
Charles P. O'Brien, M.D.
Alfred H. Stanton, M.D.*
John S. Strauss, M.D.

Ginsburg Fellows
Ira Dosovitz, M.D.—1977, 1978
James Witschy, M.D.—1979, 1980
Robert N. Golden, M.D.—1981, 1982
Kathleen M. Myers, M.D.—1983, 1984

Postfellow Guest
Ira Dosovitz, M.D., 1979-1983

*Deceased

COMMITTEE ON ADOLESCENCE
Silvio J. Onesti, Jr., Belmont, Mass.,
Chairperson
Ian A. Canino, New York, N.Y.
Harrison P. Eddy, New York, N.Y.
Sherman C. Feinstein, Highland Park, Ill.
Warren J. Gadpaille, Denver, Colo.
Michael Kalogerakis, New York, N.Y.
Clarice J. Kestenbaum, New York, N.Y.
Derek Miller, Chicago, Ill.

COMMITTEE ON AGING
Gene D. Cohen, Rockville, Md.,
Chairperson
Charles M. Gaitz, Houston, Tex.
Lawrence F. Greenleigh, Los Angeles, Calif.
Robert J. Nathan, Philadelphia, Pa.
George H. Pollock, Chicago, Ill.
Harvey L. Ruben, New Haven, Conn.
F. Conyers Thompson, Jr., Atlanta, Ga.

COMMITTEE ON CHILD PSYCHIATRY
Paul L. Adams, Galveston, Tex.,
Chairperson
James M. Bell, Canaan, N.Y.
Harlow Donald Dunton, New York, N.Y.
Joseph Fischhoff, Detroit, Mich.
Joseph M. Green, Madison, Wis.
John F. McDermott, Jr., Honolulu, Hawaii
John Schowalter, New Haven, Conn.
Theodore Shapiro, New York, N.Y.
Peter Tanguay, Los Angeles, Calif.
Lenore F.C. Terr, San Francisco, Calif.

COMMITTEE ON COLLEGE STUDENTS
Kent E. Robinson, Towson, Md.,
Chairperson
Robert L. Arnstein, Hamden, Conn.
Varda Backus, La Jolla, Calif.
Myron B. Liptzin, Chapel Hill, N.C.
Malkah Tolpin Notman, Brookline, Mass.
Gloria C. Onque, Pittsburgh, Pa.
Elizabeth Aub Reid, Cambridge, Mass.
Earle Silber, Chevy Chase, Md.
Tom G. Stauffer, White Plains, N.Y.

COMMITTEE ON CULTURAL PSYCHIATRY
Andrea K. Delgado, New York, N.Y.,
Chairperson
Edward F. Foulks, Philadelphia, Pa.
Ezra E.H. Griffith, New Haven, Conn.
Pedro Ruiz, Houston, Tex.
John P. Spiegel, Waltham, Mass.
Ronald M. Wintrob, Providence, R.I.
Joe Yamamoto, Los Angeles, Calif.

COMMITTEE ON THE FAMILY
Henry U. Grunebaum, Cambridge, Mass.,
Chairperson
W. Robert Beavers, Dallas, Tex.
Ellen M. Berman, Merion, Pa.
Lee Combrinck-Graham, Philadelphia, Pa.
Ira D. Glick, New York, N.Y.
Frederick Gottlieb, Los Angeles, Calif.
Joseph Satten, San Francisco, Calif.

COMMITTEE ON GOVERNMENTAL AGENCIES
William W. Van Stone, Palo Alto, Calif.,
Chairperson
James P. Cattell, Monterey, Mass.
Sidney S. Goldensohn, New York, N.Y.
Naomi Heller, Washington, D.C.
Roger Peele, Washington, D.C.

COMMITTEE ON HANDICAPS
Norman R. Bernstein, Chicago, Ill.,
Chairperson
Meyer S. Gunther, Chicago, Ill.
Betty J. Pfefferbaum, Houston, Tex.
William H. Sack, Portland, Oreg.
William A. Sonis, Bethesda, Md.
George Tarjan, Los Angeles, Calif.
Thomas G. Webster, Washington, D.C.
Henry H. Work, Bethesda, Md.

COMMITTEE ON INTERNATIONAL RELATIONS
Francis F. Barnes, Chevy Chase, Md.,
Chairperson
Robert M. Dorn, Sacramento, Calif.
John S. Kafka, Washington, D.C.

TABLE OF CONTENTS

RESEARCH AND THE COMPLEX
CAUSALITY OF THE SCHIZOPHRENIAS

1

INTRODUCTION

The study of the schizophrenias suffers from the problem of the extreme complexity of the phenomena under investigation. These problems range from definition of the disorder, identification of cases, and measurement of variables, to development of appropriate and rigorous research methodologies. In addition, the philosophy underlying the investigation of clinical phenomena has differed cyclically as a function of prevailing scientific values and attitudes which, at times, have emphasized biological components and, at other times, the psychosocial aspects of etiology.

Historically, natural science has progressed from direct observation to univariate analysis to multivariate analysis. During the 1930s there was increasing recognition that multivariate statistical analyses should include the interactional terms between individual variables. This emphasis on the interaction between variables led to a clearer understanding that, in complex causal systems, the whole is greater than the sum of its parts.

This report emphasizes the need for research that clarifies the pattern of relationships between biologic, psychologic, and social variables in the effort to understand better the etiologies of the schizophrenias. The report also emphasizes the necessity for interdisciplinary approaches utilizing multivariate analyses and, as they become available, new methods for the study of dynamic, open interactive systems.

A number of key terms that are often employed in different ways need clarification regarding their use in this report. The term *etiology* is used to describe any factor that contributes to the occurrence of a particular event. In referring to *domains* of research we are describing those clusters of disciplines considered to be biologic, psychologic, or social. The terms *univariate* and *multivariate* refer to statistical methods of analyzing particular types of data. Multivariate analysis allows the investigator to manipulate two or more variables simultaneously and permits the assessment of interactions. In doing so, multivariate analysis assumes a fixed and specifiable relationship between the variables being studied, differing therefore from systems analysis which does not make such an assumption. A *systems* approach assumes that the relationships between variables are dynamic and changing in response to other and frequently unaccounted for variables. However, the mathematical techniques necessary to operationalize systems concepts are only now beginning to emerge.

As a consequence of the complexity of many systems, ideas about causality have changed. Forrester (1969), for example, says that causality in complex systems can be the result of transient changes in the dominance of one or more feedback loops in a system containing many such loops. Thus, causes may exist not only in prior events but also in the structure or policies of the system. There is no necessary causal implication when two events occur sequentially in complex systems, but rather they may be coincident events without causal relationship. Bloch (1979) states that a systems perspective calls for basic change in *how* one knows. Steinglass (1978) emphasizes the switch from a reliance on deductive reasoning to one that is concerned primarily with the recognition of patterns. Weakland (1977) suggests primary attention be paid to factors that reinforce an interaction rather than those that initiate it.

Although this report emphasizes the need for cross-domain research, the need for research within a single discipline or domain continues. We do not believe, however, that either single-discipline or single-domain research can address the causation of the schizophrenias adequately. Too much evidence suggests that the etiologies of these disorders are best conceptualized in terms of multiple variables that demand examination within a biopsychosocial framework. One should not expect, for example, the geneticist, psychodynamicist, or chemist to study productively the etiologies of the schizophrenias in isolation from each other. To rely only on such strategies may even delay advances in understanding. The questions that can be addressed most profitably by single disciplines or domains are narrower in scope than the broader issue of which biologic, psychologic, and social variables, in concert, are involved in the etiologies of the schizophrenias.

A model of causality utilizing insights from multiple domains is rarely reflected in the research literature. Published studies continue to reflect a major emphasis on single-discipline or single-domain research. Whether focusing on neurochemical, developmental, or family systems variables, such studies contrast findings concerning schizophrenics and control groups as if other domains either did not exist or were of little significance. The exceptions often reflect wide variation in the manner in which different variables are considered. Variables from one discipline may be studied with refined and precise technologies whereas macroscopic techniques are used to consider other variables. For example, genetic studies exploring the prevalence of schizophrenia in genetically vulnerable individuals often use highly sophisticated genetic assessment techniques and mathematical models, but assess family characteristics on the basis of global, general measures. These studies neglect advances in family systems research that provide the investigator with more refined techniques of assessing family variables. Similarly, family investigators often focus microscopically on family systems variables, neglecting other systems or, at best, considering them only superficially.

There are many reasons for the continuing emphasis on

single-discipline or single-domain research. One reason for the tendency to think in simple causal terms is the "law" of parsimony, which states that simple is best unless a more complex approach or model can actually be demonstrated to be better. Although we believe that single-discipline or single-domain research is inadequate for understanding the origin of the schizophrenias, we cannot yet provide an adequate complex model for cross-domain approaches. Attempts to construct such models have been either mired in vagueness, metaphor, and unmanageable complexity, or marked by methodologic beauty but clinical irrelevance. Three major issues have confronted all serious considerations of more complex models of the schizophrenias:

1) *The seductiveness of single-discipline thinking.* Complex models of causality play havoc with the clinician's sense of certainty, which under some circumstances may be essential for rapid, decisive treatment. A tendency to return to simple explanations at times of trouble or doubt is consistently with us. Beyond epistemological habit, there may be a built-in psychologic mechanism or tendency to think in single-variable terms whether in ascribing causality or in the basic process of labeling and classifying (Raven, Berlin, & Breedlove, 1971). Together these forces push constantly to bring efforts at "system thinking" back to the more comfortable univariate format.

2) *The question of which variables and which models.* Opening the possibility—perhaps necessity—for complex models that cross the boundaries of disciplines and domains reveals the fearsome chaos that generally accompanies the loss of established orthodoxy. If the rules are changing, what should be considered and how? The possible complexity of variables and the number of models for combining them are practically infinite. Genetic, biochemical, family, developmental, psychophysiological, cultural, social, and many other factors have been demonstrated as important in the schizophrenias,

and each factor in itself may be complex. Reiss and Wyatt (1975), Lewis, Beavers, Gossett, and Phillips (1976), Buchsbaum and Haier (1978), Strauss, Loevsky, Glazer, and Leaf (in press), and others have suggested approaches to variable and system selection, but this issue is far from resolved.

3) *An incomplete understanding of the tensions that exist between those with either predominantly biologic or psychosocial perspectives of the schizophrenias.* This impedes serious consideration of more complex models of the schizophrenias. In agreement with Kandel (1979), we recognize that such tension not only is characteristic of the interaction between closely related fields of science, but often can result in the advancement of knowledge. Wilson (1977) emphasizes that for most major disciplines in science an antidiscipline develops, and Kandel (1979) points out that neurobiology is the new antidiscipline for dynamic psychiatry. Neurobiology can (and is) revitalizing dynamic psychiatry by forcing new methodologies and insights. However, it cannot, by itself, provide sufficiently rich models of the schizophrenias—such models require an interdisciplinary view of multiple, interacting variables. Psychiatry, dealing with complex clinical reality, must ask the questions that cross the boundaries between disciplines and domains. This view of the interchange between a clinical discipline and a basic science underlying that discipline describes how the tension may lead to advances in understanding.

In the late 1950s Caudill (1958) noted the need to study variables from different domains as they relate to issues of health and illness, and Selye (1956) introduced a complex model of disease. More recently, Dubos (1965), Bakan (1968), Cassell (1976), Moss (1973), and Weiner (1977) are among the writers who have presented more complex models of disease in general. For many years Manfred Bleuler (1941) has stressed the importance of multiple variable, longitudinal, clinical research in furthering understanding of the schizophrenias. More recently, Scheflen (1981) has proposed the basic structure of a complex model with which to understand the schizophrenias.

An example of the application of a complex model to understanding disease is that described by Engel (1977, 1979). He proposes a biopsychosocial model of disease which derives from systems theory and considers a wide range of hierarchically organized variables in interaction with each other. This model not only calls for consideration of a large group of diverse variables, but also emphasizes their hierarchical interrelationships. Each subsystem of variables interacts directly or indirectly with every other subsystem, and disturbance at one level may be contained at that level or affect all other levels. Engel suggests that the spread of disturbance through many levels is a crucial factor in the development of disease. One problem involved in the use of such models is their level of abstraction. For example, terms like "positive and negative feedback" and "homeostasis" have great appeal for considerations related to the schizophrenias, but are difficult to operationalize or test, and disappointment has followed attempts to use them.

A systems approach to the etiologies of the schizophrenias can also relate to the clinical endeavors of assessment, treatment, and prevention. Such an approach can help the clinician decide what to assess and how to combine variables in diagnosis and treatment. In a like manner, clinical information is equally crucial to the success of a systems paradigm. Given the large number of possible variables and ways of combining them, clinical information should be a major feedback loop in the continuing elaboration of the model.

The clinician's model of causality may involve at least two levels of complexity: one for acute, potentially fatal clinical events, and a second for other situations. When faced with a crisis as, for example, in patients with diabetic coma, acute myocardial infarction, or suicidal panic, the clinician must deal with the most pressing variables and intervene promptly and incisively. In these situations the threat to life is direct and immediate, and a simple, linear model may be most appropriate. The next patient seen by the clinician, however, may be an aging person with severe rheumatoid arthritis, an adolescent with labile diabetes, or a chronically depressed individual. In these situations, the role of multiple and diverse variables mandate the use of a more complex model of causality. The clinician's sense of certainty growing out of a simple cause-and-effect schema may be lost, but compensated for by the greatly increased range of interventions provided by the more complex model of disease. The ability of the clinician to move back and forth between levels, as the context demands, both requires and reflects a high level of clinical expertise.

It is against the background of these issues that this report is cast. Its primary goal is to encourage research efforts that clarify the patterns of relationships among groups of variables in various domains thought to be related to the etiologies of the schizophrenias. In pursuing this goal, we shall make the following assumptions about the schizophrenias:

1) *The assumption of heterogeneity.* This report assumes that there is a group of schizophrenias. Further, it assumes that the complex interaction of etiologic variables is different for different forms of schizophrenia. Each form displays certain characteristics that differentiate it from other forms. These characteristics may be biologic, psychologic, or social. The assumption of heterogeneity is supported by both clinical and research findings and parallels current knowledge about other disorders such as hypertension or diabetes.

2) *The assumption of illness.* This report assumes that the schizophrenias are illnesses, not alternative lifestyles. Although there may be a risk that secondary deviance might be brought about as a result of the label of schizophrenia, this report assumes that the primary disturbance of schizophrenic patients is a biopsychosocial reality.

3) *The assumption of syndrome.* This report assumes that the

present state of knowledge about the schizophrenias is consistent with the designation of syndrome. Although the terms
syndrome, reaction, illness, and disease often lack precision,
this report defines syndrome as a clinical disorder in which
there are certain patterns of symptoms, the etiology of which
is poorly or incompletely understood. It is useful, however,
to keep in mind that syndromes are composed not only of
those symptoms that various patients have in common, but
also of features that reflect individual, idiosyncratic elements.
Bowers (1974), for example, suggests that although the development of delusions is a basic feature of certain stages of
some schizophrenic syndromes, the content of delusions is
related to the individual's past experiences, underlying conflicts, developmental impasses, and other idiosyncratic elements.

4) *The assumption of temporal phases.* This report assumes
that there are discernible phases or developmental stages in
the onset and progression of the schizophrenias. These
phases differ in the various schizophrenias, but specifying
the particular phase of a particular form of schizophrenia is
an important consideration in planning research. Although
often described in the simple terms, *acute* or *chronic,* the assumptions here are that there are other phases and that each
phase may be characterized by a different combination of
biologic, psychologic, and social variables. Rheumatic heart
disease may serve as an example. The initial stage involves
a pharyngitis caused by a virulent strain of group A strep-
tococci. A small percentage of such patients develop acute
rheumatic fever. This phase may be characterized by poly-
arthritis, carditis, chorea, erythema marginatum, and sub-
cutaneous nodules. Of those patients who develop a carditis,
some also develop endocarditis. During the third phase there
is healing of these cardiac lesions and, for some patients,
fibrous thickening and adhesion of the valve commissures
resulting in the characteristic valvular deformities. The
fourth phase involves a variable period (frequently many

years) in which the patient may be asymptomatic. The fifth phase involves the development of congestive heart failure secondary to the valvular deformities. This simplified outline is a useful illustration of how the investigator wishing to study rheumatic heart disease must specify which phases of the illness are to be studied. To combine patients from all five phases might well obscure data that could clarify major aspects of the illness.

Although the temporal phases of the various schizophrenias are less clearly understood, we wish to emphasize the need to separate and study their phenomenology. To study the schizophrenias by doing research only with chronic patients may be similar to trying to understand rheumatic heart disease by studying only those patients experiencing congestive heart failure secondary to rheumatic valvular disease.

5) *The assumption of adaptive failure*. Although schizophrenia may develop in the absence of apparent stress, clinical observations suggest that a person is more prone to develop the syndrome during a period in which internal and external events are perceived subjectively as stressful. The assumption that the individual has failed to adapt to stress is difficult to define operationally, although the concept is central to many of the newer and more complex models of disease.

Understanding an illness often involves considering how individuals vary in their vulnerabilities to illness in general, their predispositions to specific illnesses, the quality and quantity of life stress, and the role of support groups such as family, friendship networks, and work groups in mitigating the impact of stressful life circumstances. From such an orientation, the schizophrenias could not be assumed to rise de novo, but rather as attempts to deal with stress, developmental impasses, or other human predicaments in a manner that is influenced significantly by overall coping capacity, genetic predispositions, developmental deviances, interpersonal support systems, and other factors. From this perspective, the development of a schizophrenic syndrome can be understood both as an adaptive failure and as a continuing attempt to master both internal and external experiences.

In summary, this report emphasizes that in the study of a complex syndrome such as the schizophrenias it is necessary to develop complex models. Models that best approximate a complex, open, interactive system are most likely to yield illuminating results. At the present time multivariate, interdisciplinary approaches appear to be the most productive and powerful means of studying such models. Systems theory holds out a promise, as yet unfulfilled, that may ultimately bring greater coherence to our understanding.

2
THE STATE OF THE FIELD

Although the schizophrenias have been a human concern since the outset of civilization, modern concepts of their nature arose in the late 19th century at the confluence of psychiatry's beginnings and medicine's defining the disease process (Klerman, 1978). Since that time, understanding of schizophrenic disorders has been influenced by changing medical viewpoints of the nature of the disease process in general. The early success of a circumscribed disease model in the understanding of infectious diseases led to an increasing emphasis on biologic factors. It was in this scientific atmosphere that Kraepelin (1921, 1962, 1968) contributed his categorization of psychiatric disorders. His focus on symptom complexes, etiology, and outcome has sometimes been associated with unsuccessful attempts to elucidate a single biologic etiology for the schizophrenias, although it is well to emphasize that such an etiology is not a requirement or constraint of Kraepelin's model.

Bleuler (1950) provided a descriptive schema for the schizophrenias which differed from Kraepelin's by emphasizing the link between phenomenology and presumed underlying psychologic processes. Bleuler's efforts suggested the importance of considering factors in at least two domains—psychologic and biologic—in understanding the etiologies of the schizophrenias. However, the problems of such a complex approach were also reflected in Bleuler's difficulties in developing and supporting a consistent theory of psychologic and biologic contributions to schizophrenia.

Another early attempt to integrate psychosocial factors

with biologic variables was the work of Meyer (1957), whose "psychobiology" had considerable influence on the field, especially in American psychiatry. However, the vast detail of assessment required by his approach and the failure to develop testable etiologic hypotheses may have contributed to the waning influence of Meyer's teachings.

Freud (1953, 1954, 1955) and his followers in the psychoanalytic movement developed theories about psychological conflicts and deficits that contributed to an understanding of the etiologies of the schizophrenias. Although they have been useful clinically, these theories have been difficult to test or elaborate from an empirical base. Some psychoanalysts such as Sullivan (1953) were centrally concerned with the schizophrenias, and they inspired a growing emphasis on the role of psychologic factors and their interactions with family relationships in the origins and treatment of the schizophrenias. This approach contrasted strikingly with Kraepelin's and had a powerful effect on etiologic theory. Although not stressing an integrated psychobiologic view of the schizophrenias, Sullivan's influence provides some paths for systematic inclusion of interpersonal and internalized social experience in an integrated model.

This historical perspective suggests some of the approaches taken in the past to understanding the etiologies of the schizophrenias. With the exception of Meyer, there has been no major proponent of an integrated, multiple systems view. Today the majority of research into the causation of the schizophrenias continues to occur in etiologic frameworks that can be seen as derivatives of earlier single-cause forms. Most often such efforts are isolated from each other.

This section selectively reviews some of the advances in research about the schizophrenias that are derived from single-domain research and emphasizes how the inclusion of variables from other disciplines and domains might have increased the yield. More comprehensive reviews of the evidence concerning the etiologies of the schizophrenias exist and are recommended to the reader wishing to pursue them (Arieti, 1974; Bellak & Loeb, 1969; Weiner, 1980). For purposes of this illustration, theories about the etiologies of the schizophrenias derived from the following disciplines will be examined: genetics, psychophysiology (including perception and cognition), biochemistry, developmental psychology, and sociology.

GENETIC THEORIES

The idea that the schizophrenias are genetically caused was in existence long before systematic studies began, as illustrated by the concept of "tainted families." More recently, systematic studies with increased methodological sophistication have evolved, resulting in greater understanding (Cancro, 1980). Consanguinity studies, beginning early in the century (Rüdin, 1916) and continuing until recently (Bleuler, 1941; Kallman, 1938; Kety, Rosenthal, Wender, Schulsinger, & Jacobson, 1975; Odegaard, 1972; Schultz, 1932; Tsuang, Crowe, Winokur, & Clancy, 1978) have demonstrated that schizophrenia runs in families. However, this fact by no means guarantees that the disorder is genetically caused. Political or religious beliefs may prevail in families for generations, yet few would suggest that such beliefs are genetically determined. Perhaps among the most interesting of the consanguinity studies are those of Karlsson (1970, 1973). He studied approximately 100 descendants of a woman born in 1735 and found that the family produced, in addition to a large number of psychotic (presumably schizophrenic) persons, a large number of talented, gifted, and successful individuals. Recent studies of children thought to be at risk (because of having one or both parents with schizophrenia) also show that some are unusually creative (Anthony, 1974). Karlsson interpreted this finding to mean that the schizophrenic syndrome is caused by one or several combinations of two genes which, in other combinations, may produce unusual talent.

Other evidence supporting the theory that the schizophrenias run in families due to genetic causes (rather than being a learned intergenerational pattern) has been obtained primarily by observing the outcome of "natural" experiments. Twin studies show a higher than expected concordance rate for schizophrenic illnesses among monozygotic twins. Concordance rates for monozygotic twins are approximately three to four times higher than for dizygotic twins (Fischer, 1974; Gottesman & Shields, 1976; Kallman, 1946; Kringlen, 1967; Pollin, Allen, Hoffer, Stabenau, & Hrubec, 1969; Slater & Shields, 1953). However, important questions are raised about the factors influencing these results. Do similar child-rearing experiences occur more with monozygotic than dizygotic twins? Does having a mirror-image sibling diminish one's ability to develop a clear, differentiated self-concept?

Adoptive studies represent other natural experiments that illuminate the causative role of genes. Concordance rates for monozygotic and dizygotic twins can be evaluated when twins are adopted and raised by different parents. Nearly half of the 27 sets of monozygotic twins separated early in life and raised apart developed concordance for the illness—a frequency similar to that of identical twins raised together by natural parents (Gottesman & Shields, 1976). This natural experiment occurs too rarely, however, to generate conclusive data. More common is the situation in which the child of a schizophrenic mother is adopted and raised by a presumably normal family. In several studies of such situations, the adopted children developed schizophrenia and other types of psychopathology with a frequency similar to that which occurs when children are raised by their schizophrenic mothers (Heston, 1966; Rosenthal, Wender, Kety, Schulsinger, Weiner, & Ostergard, 1968). Moreover, the children became ill with a greater frequency than adopted children whose biologic mothers were not schizophrenic.

In other natural experiments, the procedure has been reversed; i.e., both the natural and adoptive relatives of persons who develop a schizophrenic illness have been studied for the prevalence of schizophrenia and other types of psychopathology (Kety, Rosenthal, Wender, & Schulsinger, 1968; Kety et al., 1975; Wender, Rosenthal, & Kety, 1968; Wender, Rosenthal, Kety, Schulsinger, & Weiner, 1973, 1974). A high incidence of schizophrenic-like psychopathology has been found in the biological relatives but not in the adoptive relatives.

Although conclusions from these genetic studies are still a matter of some controversy (Lidz, Blatt, & Cook, 1981), in combination the consanguinity studies, twin comparison studies, and adoptive studies present strong presumptive evidence that a genetic factor operates within a broadly defined schizophrenic population. They bear testimony to the value of persistent, careful study within a single discipline.

However, these genetic studies raise complex questions which remain unanswered. Some of these questions are within the genetic discipline itself. For example, how does this genetic factor operate within a large sample of schizophrenic patients? Is the transmitted factor a fixed genotype whose variable, non-Mendelian expression is explained by the concept of incomplete penetrance?

Other questions concern the relationship of genetic variables to variables from other domains. Are the factors that determine penetrance internal to the individual and, therefore, relatively unaffected by environmental factors? Is the genetic factor triggered only by some specific form of environmental interaction? What is transmitted by the abnormal gene or genes? Does some subtle psychological or cognitive abnormality make the individual less able to cope with particular environments? These questions cannot be answered by epidemiologic (i.e., family incidence) studies alone, but need the inclusion of variables from other disciplines and domains.

Another important qualifier about the genetic studies

needs to be noted: 90% of schizophrenic patients do not have a first-degree relative with the illness. This strongly emphasizes the need to look for etiological variables in other domains.

Several studies illustrate the value of utilizing measures from other domains in genetic studies. Wender et al. (1968) have shown that the adoptive parents of schizophrenic patients appeared normal on some standard measures of psychopathology. However, when the Rorschach Tests of these adoptive parents were studied, they could be identified blindly and distinguished from adoptive parents of nonschizophrenic persons by the presence of certain abnormalities in communication. Likewise, Tienari (1968) presented preliminary results from an adoptive study that assesses both genetic and family variables prospectively. His results support the importance of genetic factors, but suggest that penetrance depends upon the concurrent presence of a highly disturbed family. These findings suggest two possibilities: One, that the adoptive families have a preexisting abnormality that participates in producing the schizophrenic syndromes, or two, that the presence of a schizophrenic child produces communication abnormalities or other difficulties in his or her adoptive family.

The need for a better integration of genetic information with other variables is but one example of the importance of assessing the contribution of characteristics from multiple domains in order to understand better the etiologies of the schizophrenias. To date the genetic studies have occurred largely in isolation from other domains.

THEORIES OF ABERRANT PSYCHOPHYSIOLOGIC, PERCEPTUAL, AND COGNITIVE FUNCTIONS

Many students of the etiologies of the schizophrenias have postulated some disorder of functions such as perception, memory, and cognition. Early observers such as Jung (1936),

Kraepelin (1918), and Bleuler (1950) noted that patients with the active illness manifest deficits in attention. Wohlberg and Kornetsky (1973) subsequently studied the attention of drug-free schizophrenic patients in a state of remission using the Continuous Performance Test. They found that in trials requiring vigilant attention the index subjects made significantly more errors than did matched controls. This suggests that the attention deficit is not secondary to the more flagrant symptoms of the psychotic disorder.

Other investigators, however, suggest that schizophrenic patients are *too* attentive and are unable to filter important stimuli from environmental "noise" and are, therefore, flooded by "unassimilable percepts" (McReynolds, 1960). It is postulated that such flooding produces anxiety and that the only escape is psychotic withdrawal. Shakow (1963) also suggested that schizophrenics are adequately attentive but cannot select the relevant aspects of stimuli. In a series of studies, Asarnow and his colleagues (Asarnow & MacCrimmon, 1978, 1981; Asarnow, Steffy, MacCrimmon, & Cleghorn, 1977; MacCrimmon, Cleghorn, Asarnow, & Steffy, 1980) have demonstrated that some schizophrenic patients and high-risk children manifest a deficiency of visual information processing that may be a biologic marker for one form of schizophrenia. Landau and co-workers (Landau, Buchsbaum, Carpenter, Strauss, & Sacks, 1975) demonstrated that patients with schizophrenia have average evoked potential responses that remain the same (or decrease) with increasing stimulation. Such results have led to considerable agreement about an attentional problem, but interpretations of its nature vary (Neuchterlein, 1977).

Holzman and co-workers (Holzman, Proctor, & Hughes, 1973; Holzman, Proctor, Levy, Yasillo, Meltzer, & Hurt, 1974) and Shagass and colleagues (Shagass, Amadeo, & Overton, 1974; Shagass, Roemer, & Amadeo, 1976) have demonstrated a disorder of eye movements in some schizophrenic patients. The schizophrenic person follows ("pursues") a smoothly moving object with quick jerks alternating with steady fixations. Other work suggests that the eye-tracking disorder correlates highly with evidence of thought disorder and the inability to sustain attention.

A number of investigators have postulated various types of cognitive deficits in preschizophrenic individuals. Payne (1973) described concretism, the inability to shift to abstract cognitive operations, as a characteristic of susceptible individuals. Mourer (1973) suggests that concretism is increased selectively in response to stimuli that have "strong meaning," that is, the potential to evoke a stronger affective response. Other investigators (Bauman & Murray, 1968; Koh & Kayton, 1974; Nachmani & Cohen, 1969) suggest that schizophrenic patients have a deficit of memory with regard to "recall" performance (as contrasted to "recognition" performance).

Those interested in these areas differ in their thinking as to whether these disorders are genetically determined, are caused by accidents of parturition, are learned, or arise spontaneously and randomly in the population. Differences of opinion also exist as to whether these aberrations are etiologic factors or secondary to the presence of schizophrenia. In any case, multivariate approaches must take these findings into account. For example, are the psychologic or psychophysiologic aberrations seen in index subjects shared by family members? Is the sharing due to a learned response, genetically determined, or both? Can success in treatment be measured by changes in these indices? Such studies are needed, as are conceptual bridges that could link such psychophysiologic findings, for example, to developmental theory, separation reactions, descriptive phenomenology, and genetic variables.

The research of Holzman et al. (1974) demonstrates a successful crossover from psychophysiologic variables to the genetic field. He investigated the presence of the eye-tracking abnormality in the nonpsychotic relatives of schizophrenic patients and found it to occur approximately six times more frequently in first-degree relatives (45 percent) than in the general population (seven percent). He also reports that in twin sets, one of whom was schizophrenic, 71 percent of monozygotic and 54 percent of dizygotic twins were concordant for abnormal eye tracking.

Fish and co-workers (Fish & Alpert, 1962b; Fish & Hagin, 1973; Fish, Shapiro, Halpern, & Wile, 1965) were among the first to link physiologic findings in the schizophrenias to a developmental perspective. These investigators followed a group of infants who, at age one month, manifested unstable physiologic regulatory patterns, such as vasomotor instability, faulty body temperature regulation, and low general alertness. In later childhood, a significant number of these children developed "schizophreniform" illnesses. This study, like that of Mednick (1958), suggests a relationship between the autonomic nervous system, early life experience, and the etiologies of the schizophrenias. Such studies are compelling in that they provide a biological linkage to early childrearing experiences considered critical in many psychoanalytic theories of the pathogenesis of the schizophrenias (Mednick & Schulsinger, 1968).

This selective review of psychophysiological and classical psychologic variables demonstrates the importance of single-discipline and single-domain research. Despite great productivity in these areas, however, much remains to be done to integrate these variables into a more complex model of etiology that requires an assessment of the concurrent influence of variables from other domains.

BIOCHEMICAL THEORIES

Perhaps in no discipline or domain other than biochemical research does one find so much evidence of a search for the "magic bullet" in the etiologies of the schizophrenias. While few investigators openly maintain that a single explanation can be found, the many studies of one enzyme or one abnormal serum constituent suggest the persistence of single-variable thinking. Several early "discoveries," like the "pink spot" or taraxein, tantalized investigators with the possibility of such a solution. Disorders of transmethylation or central dopamine receptor dysfunction, as current examples, tantalize in a similar fashion.

Searches for a biochemical test for the schizophrenias have utilized one or more of the following assumptions: There is an abnormal substance present, there is an abnormal sensitivity to a normal substance, or there is an abnormal amount of a normal substance. An example of the search for an abnormal substance would be the work on hemodialysis and the report of an abnormal endorphin in the dialysate fluid. The dopamine hypothesis can be considered an example of either increased sensitivity to a normal amount of a transmitter or increased production of the transmitter.

The question of which biochemical system is most likely to be involved in the etiologies of the schizophrenias is the source of much controversy, and the many possibilities are attended by the production of enormous amounts of data in studies of a wide range of biochemical substances. One of the factors expanding this area so vastly—and compounding confusion—is the question of whether a discovered biochemical aberration is part of the etiologies of the schizophrenias, is a secondary manifestation, or is simply a coexisting condition. No categorization of biochemical findings along these lines is possible at the present time.

Despite increasing sophistication of biochemical measurements, there remain serious problems of replication of reported abnormalities in the schizophrenias. Almost as soon as a new assay technique is developed, it is tried in a schizophrenic population. Usually, some deviance from normal is reported. However, when other investigators try the assay in other schizophrenic populations, either no deviation from normal or a different abnormality is reported.

The difficulty of accurate diagnosis underlies much of the failure to produce replicable findings in the schizophrenias. All research into the schizophrenias is dependent upon the gathering of patient samples that are homogeneous in meaningful ways. The biochemist's approach to this problem is to identify a pathologic biochemical mechanism and to create a test for establishing the presence or absence of that mechanism. From such findings, a disease category is fashioned that is based on a shared biochemical mechanism rather than only on shared clinical signs and symptoms. Problems involved in the lack of clinical homogeneity, however, continue to impede the success of such efforts.

Another difficulty in relating biochemical measures to more complex models of the schizophrenias is the tremendous difference in the sensitivity of measurements. While biochemical measures are capable of sensitivity at times down to 10^9gram, clinical measures involve estimates and judgments at a far less precise level of sensitivity.

Biochemical research requires an advanced state of technical knowledge, and it may be particularly easy for investigators to become so immersed in refined procedures and technical language that there is little interest in, or opportunity for, collaboration with investigators from other domains, particularly those of a less exact nature. The problems of replicability of biochemical findings in the schizophrenias may lie to a significant degree in the relative isolation from other scientific fields in which much of the research is conducted. Patient populations have rarely been studied systematically with control of pertinent nosologic subtype variables such as process–reactive, acute–chronic, paranoid–nonparanoid, and others. Biochemical studies have often been done on populations without knowledge of their homogeneity or heterogeneity concerning other parameters such as, for example, reaction times, evoked potential responses, and EEG patterns. The failure to use knowledge available from other domains has hindered the biochemical approach and may lead to the loss of important data regarding some forms of schizophrenia.

THEORIES OF ABERRANT PSYCHOLOGIC DEVELOPMENT

One major line of investigation of the etiologies of the schizophrenias—for many years the dominant strategy—has been to study the psychological development of the individual. Some of this research has focused on the individual exclusively. Other studies have focused on the individual's development within the family. These two approaches will be discussed separately. Although some research efforts in the area of individual development involve the relationship of the child to a mothering person, these studies will be discussed within the category of individual development because: 1) the primary focus is the effect of the dyadic relationship on individual development; 2) these studies rarely focus on the impact of the total family. Research regarding individual development and the family-focused studies has been almost entirely single-domain with little reference to other domains. Curiously, both the individually-focused and family-focused research strategies are also relatively isolated from each other, revealing how little crossover there is between even such closely related lines of investigation.

Childhood and adolescent development

Studies of individual development have explored several ways by which developmental variables may lead to schizophrenia. Several studies have suggested a high frequency of psychiatric problems in children whose mothers' pregnancies or deliveries were complicated by either psychologic or medical problems (Pasamanick & Knobloch, 1961; Stott & Latchford, 1978). Available evidence does not suggest that these events are specific for the later development of schizophrenia, but these studies do raise the question of nonspecific vulnerability due to neurological dysfunction resulting from stressful pregnancies, poor prenatal nutrition and care, and accidents of labor and delivery. Adding weight to this possibility is the finding of neurological abnormalities in some children with schizophrenia (Birch & Hertzig, 1967) or in some children at risk for schizophrenia (Marcus, 1973).

In another developmental approach it has been postulated that vulnerability to the schizophrenias may develop because of interference with "critical phases" of attachment between infant and mother during which reciprocal behaviors are established that bond the two in a close relationship. Although not relating specifically to the schizophrenias, Spitz's (1945) work with neonates raised in a foundling home is an early example of this theory. The neonates' only contact with mothering was "assembly-line" feeding and changing, and they demonstrated frightening rates of death, failure to thrive, or low IQs as compared to orphaned infants offered traditional rocking and nurturing. More recent and systematic studies suggest that the infant's failure to develop normal attachment behavior with both parents may be associated with the subsequent development of a wide range of behavioral abnormalities, including affective constriction, angry attacks on the mother, stereotypes, and strikingly inappropriate behaviors (Main & Weston, 1982). Whether such children are at increased risk for the subsequent development of schizophrenia is yet to be ascertained.

Several studies have shown that early parental separation and loss are predictive of later development of serious psychiatric disorders including—but not specifically—schizophrenia (Garmezy & Streitman, 1974). Sullivan (1953) theorized that schizophrenic individuals had been predisposed to their illnesses by their mothers' excessive anxiety which interfered with growth-facilitating mother-child attachment. Fromm-Reichmann (1948) extended this concept by defining a "schizophrenogenic" mother. These investigations, as well as others (Ainsworth, 1964, 1970; Bowlby, 1969; Klaus, Jerauld, Kreger, McAlpine, Steffa, & Kennell, 1972; Sander, 1962), suggest that dysfunctional bonding and attachment may be relevant to the pathogenesis of some types of schizophrenia.

In another vein, Thomas and others (Bridger, 1961; Lipton, Steinschneider, & Richmond, 1965; Thomas, Birch, Chess, Hertzig, & Korn, 1965; Thomas & Chess, 1977) have offered evidence that infants differ constitutionally. Thomas's group classified nine "temperamental types." Although their studies do not suggest a clear cause of these constitutional differences, longitudinal observation of the children has revealed that some temperamental types are more vulnerable to a spectrum of psychopathology, including childhood schizophreniform illness. Most investigators conducting these studies emphasize that such vulnerability must be understood in an interactional context. Some mothers may be effective in nurturing one temperamental type but not another. Bergman and Escalona (1949) postulated, for example, that some infants are excessively sensitive to a variety of sensory inputs which disrupt the evolution of ego functions and make them more vulnerable to psychosis. Similar work by Fish has been referred to earlier (Fish & Alpert, 1962b; Fish & Hagin, 1973; Fish et al., 1965).

Mahler, Pine, and Bergman (1975) offer further leads about the role of deviations in the developmental process that may be related to the etiologies of the schizophrenias. Their work extends observations of early development from the initial bonding process to the graduated alteration of the early bond. Central to this process is the achievement of a cognitive step called "object constancy" by which the child can call upon an internalized image of the mother and the previous nurturing relationship with her. Mahler et al. (1975) postulated that the person who later develops schizophrenia never achieves object constancy. Most psychoanalytic theorists agree that some adolescents or adults who are vulnerable to psychotic states have a deficit in such object constancy.

Any theory of the etiologies of the schizophrenias needs to take into account the frequent onset of the syndrome in adolescence and young adulthood. Because the demands in these phases of development for individuation, increasing socialization, and determination of life direction are stressful, the fragile coping mechanisms of vulnerable individuals may be overwhelmed.

Virtually all studies of individual development, including most of the above studies, constitute single-domain research. Such studies generally do not consider other domains except in passing, as in reference to certain "constitutional proclivities." One exception that suggests the fertility of a cross-domain approach is a study by Mednick (1958) investigating the possibility that some disorders of autonomic arousal may be the precursor of the schizophrenic syndrome. Mednick theorized that predisposition to the illness is based upon a habituated autonomic over-responsiveness to mild stress which becomes so pervasive over time that it interferes with the developing perceptual and cognitive abilities. He and Schulsinger (1968) added credibility to this idea by showing that the galvanic skin response (as their measure of autonomic responsiveness) of children at risk for schizophrenia (because they had schizophrenic mothers) was, on the average, more deviant than for children of normal mothers. The children in the risk sample who subsequently had greater psychopathology also had more abnormal galvanic skin responses and more frequent periods of extended separation from their mothers than did children at risk who grew up healthy. Further cross-domain studies of this sort are obviously needed.

Development within the family

A second major area of developmental studies relates to the influence of the family. In the late 1940s, investigators began to study systematically the characteristics of families containing a schizophrenic member. Ruth and Theodore Lidz (1949) carried out one of the first such studies. They compared the characteristics of families containing either schizophrenic or depressed members utilizing a retrospective chart review. This study focused attention on the role of family variables in the etiologies of the schizophrenias and was a factor in the subsequent development of interactional approaches to the study of the family as well as adding impetus to the early development of family therapy. Bateson and colleagues (Bateson, Jackson, Haley, & Weakland, 1956) noticed an unusual pattern of pathological communication between mother and patient in which the mother communicated contradictory implicit and explicit messages that posed a paralyzing dilemma. The father's inactivity in such families offered the patient no help, and the patient was not able to escape the dilemma. Bateson and his group hypothesized that recurrent exposure of a child to such "double-binding" communication either caused or contributed to the schizophrenic state.

Kafka (1971) critically evaluated the double-bind theory and suggested that rather than overexposure to such paradoxical communications, the vulnerable family member is underexposed to ambiguous communications during certain developmental stages. He suggests that this is due to parental fear and intolerance of ambiguity and that the underexposure leads to the child's subsequent inability to tolerate ambiguity and deal with the paradoxical aspects of reality.

Other investigators began to look for unclear communication or other problems in the parental relationship that might confuse a young developing person. Lidz and co-workers (Lidz, Cornelison, Fleck, & Terry, 1957; Lidz, Cornelison, Terry, & Fleck, 1958) noted major disturbances in the parental relationship. Bowen (1960) theorized that problems in the parental relationship might have an ego-disorganizing effect on a developing child, and he specifically hypothesized that a state of parental "emotional divorce" impaired normal development. Wynne and Singer and their colleagues (Wynne & Singer, 1963a, 1963b; Wynne, Singer, Bartko, & Toohey, 1975) noted deviant styles of communicating thoughts and feelings within such families and described strong correlations between parental "communication deviance" and the severity of symptoms in adolescent offspring diagnosed as schizophrenic.

Taking a more general approach, Lewis and his colleagues (1976) developed rating scales measuring 13 family variables found to be measures relevant to the competence of family functioning. They used this scale to rate families along a continuum ranging from severely dysfunctional to extremely competent. Extremely competent families consistently produce autonomous, socially competent adolescent offspring. Schizophrenic adolescents are found in families with the most dysfunctional scores with regard to the 13 variables.

Critics of family studies raise methodological issues—especially that of studying families after schizophrenia has become manifest—and insist that no clear evidence exists that problems within families are either a necessary or sufficient cause for the schizophrenic syndrome. More to our point, these earlier studies have been directed solely at studying family variables separate from the role of variables from other domains. In contrast, several recent studies have been carried out that relate family variables to other domains. Brown and his co-workers (Brown, Birley, & Wing, 1972), for example, have developed the Camberwell Interview to assess several aspects of a parent's attitude towards a schizophrenic child. They found that families characterized by overinvolvement, hostility, and criticism directed at the patient—the high "expressed emotion" (EE) group—provide a home environment that markedly increased the likelihood of relapse in discharged schizophrenic patients.

Of greater relevance to this report has been the effort to show the relationship of this family variable, high EE, not only to the course of the disorder, but also to treatment interventions. Vaughn and Leff (1976) first showed that

drugs can decrease relapse rates when administered to schizophrenic patients returning to high EE families. In contrast,
the drugs appear to have no effect on relapse (at nine months
following hospital discharge) for those patients who return
to families rated low on EE. More recently, both Falloon
(Falloon & Lieberman, 1983) and Leff (Leff, Berkowitz, &
Kuipers, 1983) have shown that family interventions directed
at reducing the high EE can decrease relapse rates dramat-
ically.

As another example of cross-domain research, Leff (1976)
has shown that schizophrenic persons in high EE families
have a heightened autonomic responsivity compared to those
in low EE families. These studies are outstanding in illus-
trating the complex interactions between social context, treatment effect, and psychophysiologic variables.

SOCIOCULTURAL THEORIES

The impact of cultural and broad environmental variables
has been particularly difficult to explore rigorously. However, a biopsychosocial model of disease necessitates consideration of sociocultural variables. These broad areas may be
the richest veins yet to be mined, particularly as sociologic
and epidemiologic methods become more sophisticated.

A central question concerns whether the prevalence of the
schizophrenias changes across national boundaries, among
races, and over long periods of time. The available evidence
indicates that the schizophrenias are ubiquitous and do not
appear to occur with significantly different prevalences in
different cultures, nations, or races (Goldhamer & Marshall,
1953). Some studies have suggested that national origin may
influence the type of symptoms in affected individuals, but
prevalences remain remarkably similar (Opler & Singer,
1956). There is, however, growing evidence that the course
of schizophrenic illnesses is more benign in nonindustrial

societies (Satorious, Jablensky, & Shapiro, 1977) and in reporting a study in Sri Lanka, Waxler (1979) has discussed the ways in which family structure, multiple treatment systems, and systems of belief may account for the lessened prevalence of chronicity.

A related question, also dealing with various social environments, is whether prevalences change over long periods of time. The answer is uncertain because of reporting difficulties and the changing diagnostic systems used during various historical periods. However, references to psychotic, presumably schizophrenic, individuals such as the man possessed in the Apostle Mark's tale of the Gadarene swine (Mark 5:9) have been common since human existence has been recorded.

Clearly, stress can arise from many sources within a person's environment, and such stress increases individual vulnerability to illness (Brown & Birley, 1968; Holmes & Rahe, 1967; Paykel, Prusoff, & Myers, 1975; Rahe, Mahan, Arthur, & Gunderson, 1970; Selye, 1956). A number of investigators (Brown & Birley, 1968; Jacobs & Myers, 1976; Rogler & Hollingshead, 1965) have demonstrated that schizophrenic patients experienced more stressful life events preceding their illnesses than socioeconomically matched normal controls. Also focusing on environmental variables, several studies (Malzberg & Less, 1956; Odegaard, 1932) have implicated crosscultural migration as a stress that increases the prevalence of the schizophrenias. These studies show a higher rate of illness in emigrants than in those who remain in their place of birth.

Research on socioeconomic variables has shown that being poor is correlated with a higher prevalence of schizophrenia (Clark, 1948; Faris & Dunham, 1939; Hollingshead & Redlich, 1958). Some authors suggest that poor persons' abilities to cope with stress are diminished (Langer & Michael, 1963). A higher prevalance of schizophrenia in the lowest social class in large cities has been demonstrated, although this finding diminishes when studying cities of less than 500,000 population (Clausen & Kohn, 1959).

Such findings about social class raise perplexing questions. Do people with schizophrenia drop into lower social classes because of their various disabilities? Or do poor and disorganized neighborhoods increase the chance of a person's becoming schizophrenic because of higher rates of reproductive casualties, the lack of availability of good general health care and nutrition, the lack of social supports, or other characteristics of such neighborhoods? These questions cannot be answered at present, but even a brief review suggests that both socioeconomic and urban geographic variables have impact on the pathogenesis of the schizophrenias. Such reports, by themselves, however, are limited. The studies of socioeconomic variables, for example, have not involved family characteristics in order to understand whether being poor remains a risk factor when controlled for family competence. Many treatment studies examine socioeconomic status only as a variable to be controlled, rather than examining its relationship to treatment, course, and outcome.

Cross-domain research involving sociocultural variables might be very fruitful, but it has been rare. One example in the realm of theoretical linkage is Murphy's catalog of studies in which changes in the incidence of schizophrenia over time correlate with stressful changes in social conditions such as war, geographic displacement, or role definitions (Murphy, 1967). He develops a theory of the nature of stresses that are evocative of schizophrenia and cites four qualities of such stresses: 1) the stress demands an unlearned response, 2) the stress is perceived as important, 3) there is no simple solution, and 4) it is chronic. He elaborates on these criteria by noting that the stress demands action or at least decisions by the individual and that the correct (i.e., satisfying) action is difficult to recognize because of the complexity or ambiguity of the information available. Under these circumstances, Murphy feels that the incidence of schizophrenia can increase two- or threefold, but rarely more. There is an obvious parallel between these defining characteristics of the cultural stressors evocative of schizophrenia and the double-bind theory of families of schizophrenic individuals.

3

EXAMPLES OF INTERDISCIPLINARY CROSS-DOMAIN RESEARCH

ASSUMPTIONS

Interdisciplinary, cross-domain research on the etiologies of the schizophrenias has been influenced by a number of assumptions about how such research should be conducted. Some have supportive evidence and seem warranted, while others may not be legitimate. Although these assumptions have not been assessed systematically, they have dominated the approach to cross-domain studies.

The first assumption is that such studies must be large and expensive and that they require long-term collaboration and a huge interdisciplinary staff. Since the size of a particular study is related to the hypotheses being tested, the model of the schizophrenias guiding the inquiry, and other factors, large size can be either a potential hazard or a potential strength. One hazard is that massive data collection can consume so much energy that prodigious amounts of data may be generated without many analyses actually being completed. Although recent developments in the computer sciences provide the investigators with a much more rapid and efficient approach to data analysis, the problems of synthesis and interpretation may remain formidable.

Large studies also require mechanisms that increase the likelihood of interaction between investigators who represent the different domains. When a truly collaborative process evolves (and the problems are legion), investigators are more likely to use data from other domains in ways that increase the yield.

A second and related assumption involves the amount and length of time required to accomplish interdisciplinary cross-domain studies. Often the necessary time is underestimated, exhausting funds and leaving data analysis incomplete. Unless an interdisciplinary team is already in place, considerable time is required to create the mechanisms necessary for the evolution of a stable and collaborative organization. Frequent meetings and periodic reviews are required both to increase the likelihood of collaboration and to maintain the central focus of the interdisciplinary effort.

A third assumption is that highly polished measurement techniques and advanced multivariate statistical approaches can reduce the need for clinically relevant and carefully considered hypotheses. Such substitution of technology for thought is seen often in what has been called the "shotgun" approach: A large number of variables are measured and factor analytic techniques are used to search for statistically significant relationships. This approach has not substantially enhanced our understanding of the schizophrenias.

A fourth assumption is that the conceptual and logistic problems of interdisciplinary, cross-domain research have, for the most part, been solved and will not, therefore, impede the progress of the investigation. Conversely, there are those who believe that the inherent problems are too great to be solved. Neither of these assumptions is warranted. Despite our belief that interdisciplinary, cross-domain research will advance understanding of the schizophrenias, we wish to emphasize that both conceptual and logistic problems will be encountered; many of these appear solvable if adequate efforts are made. Many of the same difficulties arise in each such project, but this problem could be minimized by developing a small group of investigators from each of the three domains (biologic, psychologic, social) to address and to clarify these recurring issues.

SELECTED STRATEGIES

Before discussing specific strategies, it appears appropriate to address the issue of the role of theoretical models in the study of the schizophrenias. The limited scope of current knowledge regarding the etiologies of the schizophrenias should encourage the continued development of multiple models. The philosopher of science, Kaplan (1976), underscored the dangers of working with too few models that are too much alike. He stressed the manner in which a single model restricts the range of conceptualizations. Models are but tentative theoretical structures designed to integrate existing data and to uncover new relationships between variables. A model is constructed, then discarded or modified as the hypotheses evolving from the model produce experimental data incongruent with the model itself.

Our suggestions regarding the appropriate models for increasing understanding of the schizophrenias are that they be consonant with clinical observations, include variables from biology, psychology, and sociology, and take into account the interaction between such variables. Use of models that are restricted to a single domain underestimates the complexity of the schizophrenias. This is true whether the domain is biologic (e.g., the dopamine hypothesis), psychologic (e.g., the schizophrenogenic mother), or social (e.g., the double-bind family interaction hypothesis). By neglecting variables from other domains, single-domain models are ultimately found to be inadequate and are discarded. In that process, data from a single domain that are crucial to the understanding of one form of the schizophrenias or one stage of a particular form may be lost.

Selection of subjects

Data with which to explore the kinds of models we suggest can be collected through the use of several strategies. One approach involves studying persons at unusually high risk for the disorder—for example, children from families with high genetic loading for the schizophrenias or children whose parents are schizophrenic. This approach has generated data that have increased our understanding of the schizophrenias, but could be complemented by other approaches to the definition of high-risk samples. Within the biologic domain, there is evidence of increased risk for children who have autonomic instability and attention deficits. In the social and psychologic domains, family characteristics such as chaotic interaction patterns, blunted affective styles, and idiosyncratic parental thinking have also been associated with an increased risk of schizophrenia. Low social class has also been associated with increased risk. More interdisciplinary research within each domain and more studies across domains can be profitable in developing a more comprehensive definition of persons at risk for the schizophrenias.

The recent report from the Rochester longitudinal study illustrates this point (Sameroff, Seifer, & Zax, 1982). At 30 months the children of chronically schizophrenic mothers were more developmentally disabled in comparison to the children of mothers who were not mentally ill. However, the offspring of schizophrenic mothers were not so disabled as the children of neurotically depressed mothers. Indeed, broad developmental disabilities were more strongly correlated with lower socioeconomic status and the chronicity and severity of the mothers' illnesses than they were with the maternal diagnoses. Although the children of the schizophrenic mothers may yet develop disabilities, the authors suggest that the definition of a high-risk sample should comprehend the combination of severe, prolonged maternal emotional disturbance, unstable family organization, poor economic circumstances, and low social status. Doane, West, Goldstein, Rodnick, & Jones (1981), have reported that measures of parental communication deviance combined with a measure of parental negative affective style measured five

years earlier predict the subsequent development of schizophrenia or schizophrenia-related disorders in nonpsychoti-
cally disturbed adolescents. This work suggests that such
family variables may be highly specific risk factors for some
forms of schizophrenia. It needs replication, particularly with
studies including variables from other domains.

Selection of variables

A second group of strategies for cross-domain research is
concerned with the selection and measurement of variables.
At the minimum, the investigator primarily concerned with
variables within one domain needs to control for critical variables in other domains. Symptom pattern, premorbid adjustment, and social class will regularly need to be controlled.
However, as our understanding of the heterogeneity of the
schizophrenias increases, other variables will need to be mon-
itored as well. Recent additions, for example, might include
cerebral ventricular size and family environment.

Using control variables of this type will be facilitated by the
development of standardized measures for each variable in
each domain. Such measures include not only the diagnostic
typologies found in DSM-III, but dimensional scales as well.
Scales measuring characteristics ranging from individual premorbid adjustment to family competence will be required.
The construction of such scales should consider the issues of
clarity, replicability, and theoretical and clinical relevance.
For example, scales providing interval data do not necessarily
imply linear relationships to the other variables being studied.
Blood pressure, for example, is measured on an interval
scale, but its pathologic implications are not linear. There is
a geometric increase in pathogenicity at each successive interval above a certain threshold. Scales to measure variables
relevant to the etiologies of the schizophrenias might need
to be considered in a similar fashion.

The relevance of particular scales depends on the specific

characteristics of the variables they seek to measure. Which measurement approach will have the greatest chance of being relevant can usually be clarified best by an investigator in that specific area. Although current knowledge suggests that the control of certain variables must be almost automatic, it is well to emphasize that such automatic consideration may, in some instances, provide false reassurance that the variable being assessed is measured adequately.

The selection and measurement of variables raise the issue of the sole reliance on diagnosis. Besides diagnosis, the severity and duration of the schizophrenic syndrome being studied need careful control. Scales are available that can help in controlling such variables, and the data from the Rochester longitudinal study (Sameroff et al., 1982) are but one example of the problems that may be encountered if the investigator assumes that all subjects fulfilling the criteria for a particular diagnosis represent the same level of psychopathology.

Another important strategy concerns whether a variable is constant or intermittent. State phenomena may vary with exacerbations or remission of the illness. Trait phenomena may remain generally constant. Knowledge of the constancy or irregularity of autonomic responsiveness, parental involvement, and other variables may make useful contributions to our understanding of the etiologies of the schizophrenias.

The desirability of focusing on interactions among variables over time is obvious, but perhaps easy to overlook. Recent advances in knowledge concerning subtle mother-neonate interactions, for example, have significantly augmented our understanding of the infant's early development in ways that could not have arisen if the investigative focus had been on either mother or infant and excluded their interaction.

It is desirable to include treatment response as an important variable to be measured in a variety of investigations. Some aspects of response to psychotropic agents, for example, are relatively easy to measure and can be included without great expenditure of effort. Whenever possible, there should be correlations with variables from other domains in ways that clarify interactions that may have immediate treatment implications.

Another strategy in the selection of variables involves the need to note variables specific to the etiologies of the schizophrenias as contrasted with those variables that operate at the more general level of increasing the probability of a variety of psychiatric syndromes. Whether, for example, characteristics such as level of family competence, lowered platelet MAO, or disturbances in mother-infant attachment behavior are associated with increased vulnerability to the schizophrenias in particular or psychopathology in general may be a crucial issue in selecting variables for a particular study.

Feasibility

Another group of strategies concern feasibility, which often determines and limits research designs. Simple and inexpensive measurements are seductive because they are easy to collect and readily replicable. However, their relevance may be minimal.

Longitudinal designs

Finally, we wish to recommend a specific strategy that involves emphasis on a particular research approach in cross-domain studies. An understanding of the etiologies of the schizophrenias seems most likely to be increased by a stronger emphasis on longitudinal and developmental research designs. In studying individuals and families over time, there is a stronger motivation to include variables from all three domains. An example of this concept is the longitudinal study of Harvard sophomores designed in the late 1930s (Vaillant, 1977). Although not concerned with the schizophrenias, the design called for studying the subjects from multiple perspectives, and this factor has produced a richer understanding of the variables that affected the subjects' lives. That certain perspectives (e.g., somatotypes) became outdated and of little value seems inevitable in longitudinal research. That certain measures (e.g., EEG) were found to predict little of subjects' subsequent life trajectories is a valuable, though negative, finding.

A particular strength of longitudinal designs for cross-domain research is their capacity to provide information on the interactional sequences of critical variables. Such an approach can help to clarify patterns, such as the relationship between early developmental disturbances and later developmental impasses or regressions occurring after periods of considerable latency. An example outside the field of schizophrenia is reported by Elder (1979) regarding the correlation of disturbance in adolescent boys' self-image and self-esteem with much earlier family realignments subsequent to the Great Depression, fathers' job losses, and mothers' increased centrality in the family. The development of the adolescents' problems was influenced by gender (only boys were affected) and age (only boys who were very young at the time of the family stress and realignment were affected). If the boys' parents had warm, supportive relationships prior to the family stress and were able to maintain their marital cohesion, the boys were protected from disturbance in self-image and self-esteem. These relationships between marital and family variables, life stress, and sons' adolescent development could be clarified only by longitudinal research. The question of which variables precede others is crucial to our understanding of the schizophrenias, and longitudinal research utilizing variables from the three domains may untangle causal interactions that are impossible to understand with other designs.

However, cross-domain longitudinal studies are extraordinarily difficult: adequate sample size, the commitment required of the investigators, the procedures required to provide stability to an interdisciplinary research team, and funding are but a few of the obvious problems. Despite such problems, we believe that a greater emphasis on a longitudinal perspective will increase our understanding of the schizophrenias. Such studies still need, of course, to be balanced by shorter-term, cross-sectional designs that help to clarify the relationships among variables at a given time, either within a single domain or across several domains.

4

APPROACHES TO CROSS-DOMAIN RESEARCH

Some approaches to cross-domain research are illustrated by the following brief research vignettes. The first three examples are described from the perspective of a biologic investigator, a family investigator, and a psychodynamic investigator. The fourth example illustrates the desirability of cross-domain studies within a longitudinal or developmental framework. A prerequisite for cross-domain studies is a finding within one domain that is reproducible and characteristic of at least one subgroup of schizophrenic patients. Armed with this finding, the investigator then includes selected variables from other disciplines and domains in order to increase the probability of identifying diverse variables and their interactions operative in the etiology of a particular form of schizophrenia.

A BIOLOGIC RESEARCH STUDY

Metabolic abnormalities and the schizophrenias

One area of research that has attracted persistent attention is the search for metabolic abnormalities in the schizophrenias. Targets of such research have included possible abnormal neurotransmitter metabolites, particularly endogenous hallucinogens. Quantitative or qualitative alterations in genetically controlled enzymes might account for the intermittent production of such hallucinogens.

One problem involved in elucidating the possible etiologic

role of such metabolites is that various studies have conflict-ing findings. As one example, several researchers (Murray, Oon, Rodnight, Birley, & Smith, 1979; Rodnight, Murray, Oon, Brockington, Nicholls, & Birley, 1976) report increased excretion of the hallucinogen dimethyltryptamine (DMT) in psychosis, while others (Carpenter, Fink, Narasimhachari, & Himwich, 1975) find no difference between schizophrenic patients and normal subjects. Although differences in bio-chemical techniques may explain these conflicting reports, much of the variance may be accounted for by the interaction of psychological or social variables with the abnormal met-abolic process. The studies have grouped patients solely on the basis of diagnosis or current symptoms which alone pro-vides insufficient differentiation among potential subgroups of schizophrenic patients. The importance of endogenous hallucinogens or other metabolic variables in some forms of schizophrenia may thus be lost.

In a cross-domain approach the biologic investigator who has identified a group of schizophrenic subjects with an ab-normal metabolite might next consider other biologic factors, such as genetic loading or diet, then select specific psycho-social variables from other domains. In this example, we sug-gest that variables such as genetic loading, family competence, life stress, and treatment response might be productive fac-tors to include. A series of preliminary questions could be asked. Examples are: Do schizophrenic subjects with an ab-normal metabolite demonstrate genetic loading for schizo-phrenia? Are they members of families that share particular interactional characteristics? Are their psychotic episodes as-sociated with high levels of life stress? Do they respond to certain psychotropic agents? Are they accessible to particular psychotherapeutic modalities?

More specific hypotheses could be tested, for example, that schizophrenic subjects with high genetic loading for schizo-phrenia, from families with relatively high levels of family competence, who experience high levels of life stress prior to the onset of psychotic symptomatology will demonstrate the highest levels of the abnormal metabolite. Further, one could hypothesize that such subjects will respond to phenothiazines, but will be difficult to engage in traditional forms of individual psychotherapy.

In testing the hypotheses, the criteria for inclusion must be considered carefully. In this example subjects should be included only if they have a DSM-III diagnosis of Schizophrenic Disorder for two years or more, have been free of neuroleptic drugs for at least two weeks, have a normal CAT scan, and demonstrate the absence of exogenous hallucinogenic drugs in the urine and the absence (by history) of the use of such drugs during the preceding month.

Each independent variable could be arranged in scalar form. Genetic variables can be rated by assessing the degree of genetic loading for schizophrenia. Approaches to obtaining reliable genetic data and defining genetic loading are far from settled issues. At the minimum, specific questions must be addressed as, for example, how is schizophrenia in relatives to be determined? Should both first- and second-degree relatives be included? What other diagnoses in relatives should be counted as part of the index of genetic loading?

Even within an otherwise homogeneous sample of schizophrenic patients, considerable variation in the duration and severity of the schizophrenic syndrome can be expected. Scales to measure duration and severity can be used to assess their relationship to other independent variables as well as to the dependent variables.

Family system variables can be assessed in a similar manner. One possibility would be measuring the level of family competence (Lewis et al., 1976) with a global rating of the family's level of psychological functioning. Measures of life stress can be quantified using available scales (Holmes & Rahe, 1967) for stressors operating during a fixed period prior to either illness onset or hospitalization.

Treatment-response variables also may be important as

they relate to the biologic dependent variable. Whether or not the subject has improved promptly with neuroleptics during prior psychotic periods and whether relapses occur if neuroleptic treatment is stopped can both be rated in scalar form. Participation in psychotherapy can be rated along a number of dimensions as, for example, attendance, accessibility for a working alliance, and therapist's status reports.

The dependent variable chosen for this brief example is the urinary excretion of an abnormal metabolite, an endogenous hallucinogen. The major difference between this example and earlier published studies is the use of a small number of specific variables from biologic, psychologic, and social domains as independent variables. Multivariate regression analyses permit a determination of the contribution of each independent variable to the measure of the dependent variable. Such analyses could both clarify the nature of specific subgroups of schizophrenic patients and lead to more focused and specific hypotheses to be tested in subsequent investigations.

A FAMILY SYSTEMS RESEARCH STUDY

Family systems and the schizophrenias

The investigator in the area of family systems also needs to consider ways in which nonfamily variables may increase understanding of the role of family factors in the etiologies of the schizophrenias. Reiss (1975), for example, reported that there had been no investigations into the etiologies of the schizophrenias published by a family researcher that focused on the interaction of family and nonfamily variables.

Several conceptual issues may have impeded progress in understanding the etiologic role of family variables. One issue is the need for clarification regarding the role of family variables specific to the development of the schizophrenias as opposed to the development of psychopathology in general.

A second issue is the need for distinction between family variables that may predispose, those that may precipitate, or those that sustain schizophrenic disorders. Finally, there is the crucial issue of heterogeneity. Family variables may play a significant role in the etiology of some forms of schizophrenia, but not in others. Research designs that include nonfamily variables should clarify the role of family variables.

As an example, the family investigator interested in the relationships of family competence to schizophrenia could include in the research design other family variables such as parental communication deviance and family expressed emotion (EE). Nonfamily psychologic variables might include a measure of the process-reactive dimension of the index subject's schizophrenic syndrome and a measure of life stress. Biologic variables could include genetic loading for schizophrenia, the presence or absence of cerebral atrophy, and platelet MAO.

These nonfamily psychologic and biologic variables are chosen as the independent variables to predict specific aspects of the family structure of schizophrenic patients. For example, the family investigator who identifies two different types of families containing schizophrenic persons—one group comprised of rigid, dominant-submissive dysfunctional families and another group comprised of even more dysfunctional, chaotic families—could, through the inclusion of nonfamily variables, increase understanding of the importance of family factors in the schizophrenias. For example, patients with a high genetic loading for schizophrenia, evidence of cerebral atrophy, low platelet MAO, high process scores on a process-reactive scale, and low levels of life stress could be predicted to be members of severely dysfunctional, chaotic families demonstrating high levels of parental communication deviance, but low levels of family expressed emotion (EE). Secondly, schizophrenic patients with no genetic loading for schizophrenia, no evidence of cerebral atrophy, normal platelet MAO, and a highly reactive onset of illness associated with high levels of life stress could be predicted to be members of rigid, moderately dysfunctional families with, however, no evidence of parental communication deviance, but with high levels of family EE.

In testing these hypotheses, the family investigator needs to be explicit and clear about the inclusion criteria. Young adult patients fulfilling the DSM-III criteria for a Schizophrenic Disorder of two or more years duration would be the major inclusion criteria. However, in this example it would be best to limit the sample to young adult patients of similar social class who are living with intact families of origin, despite the subsequent limitations imposed on the generalizations possible from such sample selection.

The independent variables in this example would be nonfamily variables associated with different forms of schizophrenia. Genetic loading would be ascertained through the use of standard, structured interviews. The presence or absence of cerebral atrophy would be determined by the use of CAT scans. Platelet MAO would be assessed by the use of standard assays.

The individual psychologic variables might include a measure of the process-reactive dimension of each subject's schizophrenic syndrome (Gossett, Meeks, Barnhart, & Phillips, 1976) and a conventional measure of life stress (Holmes & Rahe, 1967) for a fixed period preceding either illness onset or hospitalization.

The dependent variables in this example would be a small number of family variables. Family competence is considered as a family variable that predisposes to family members' psychopathology (Lewis et al., 1976). Two levels of family competence (more specifically, levels of family dysfunction) would be particularly pertinent: moderately dysfunctional, or rigid, families and severely dysfunctional, or chaotic, families.

A second family variable, a measure of parental communication deviance (Wynne et al., 1975) will be considered as a specific factor predisposing to a type of schizophrenic disorder.

A final dependent variable will be a measure of family expressed emotion (EE) that has been demonstrated to have predictive power regarding relapse in schizophrenic patients (Leff, 1976; Leff & Vaughn, 1980; Vaughn & Leff, 1976). High levels of family EE will be considered a variable that sustains a family member's schizophrenic disorder.

In this type of family research, the inclusion of nonfamily variables can lead to a better understanding of the ways in which family variables may play a variety of roles in predisposing, precipitating, or sustaining certain types of schizophrenic disorders in family members. In particular, the patterns of interaction of family and nonfamily variables could illuminate additional, more specific hypotheses to be tested in subsequent investigations.

A PSYCHODYNAMIC RESEARCH STUDY

Symbiosis and the schizophrenias

The investigator whose primary interest is psychodynamics can further understanding of the role of such factors in the etiologies of the schizophrenias by designing investigations that include variables from other disciplines and domains. In the following example, the role of symbiosis in the etiologies of the schizophrenias is explored.

The concept of symbiosis, developed in studies of early child development, describes that period in which the child is intensely and dependently attached to its object world while still unable to discriminate the boundary of self from that of the object. This concept has been applied to adult schizophrenia, most notably by Searles (1965) who posited that a developmental impasse in the symbiotic phase was pivotal in the development of adult schizophrenia and was essential in understanding the transference relationship that develops between adult schizophrenics and therapists in the course of intensive psychotherapy. From a developmental perspective, as well as from the viewpoint of psychotherapy process, the visible features of a symbiosis include an intense dependency upon the object for gratification of unspoken wants which are experienced as needs by the child or patient.

The pathogenic significance of symbiosis is also postulated to be evident in the relationships of some adult schizophrenics to their families of origin (Bowen, 1960; Ricks & Nameche, 1966; Stierlin, 1975). In the examination of such families, it was observed that the schizophrenic child and one parent (usually the mother, but sometimes the father) (Cheek, 1965) could be seen to be intensely overinvolved with all aspects of each other's life to the relative exclusion of other relationships. In the treatment situation, this took the form of overt, explicit resistance to the separation issues of adolescence as introduced by hospitalization or therapy. More recently, Arieti (1974) noted that in his clinical experience only about 25 percent of schizophrenic patients came from families in which such a symbiotic attachment could be observed.

This example represents an effort to identify this subgroup of schizophrenic patients and to test a variety of hypotheses directed at differentiating them from other groups of schizophrenic patients in whom different pathogenic pathways would be expected to operate.

At the most general level, the hypothesis to be tested states that schizophrenic subjects with symbiotic attachments to one or both parents can be discriminated from "nonsymbiotic" schizophrenic subjects on the basis of genetic loading for schizophrenia, past history, autonomic responsivity, failure to respond to subliminal stimulation, response to hospital and psychotherapeutic interventions, and treatment course and outcome.

Specifically, a series of hypotheses could be tested at three stages of this project. The dependent variables will involve two forms of Schizophrenic Disorders, symbiotic and nonsymbiotic. The subjects will be evaluated by the use of special interviews to ascertain whether they have a symbiotic or nonsymbiotic form of schizophrenia. The interviews will involve the subjects, subjects and parents, and parents, and judgments will be made of whether each subject has a symbiotic form or nonsymbiotic form of schizophrenia. The interviews on which the judgments will be made will occur prior to treatment interventions.

Once this distinction is made, the investigator would include variables from other disciplines and domains. The series of illustrative hypotheses are, in concert, aimed at clarifying further the symbiotic-nonsymbiotic distinction by including nonpsychodynamic variables in the research design.

The first group of hypotheses involves the relationship of certain baseline independent variables to the form of the schizophrenic disorder: that is, symbiotic or nonsymbiotic schizophrenia.

Two hypotheses, based on the theory that a symbiotic attachment will augment compliance with parental authority figures in the school situation but will diminish peer activities, are that past history of better school attendance and achievement will predict symbiotic schizophrenia and that past history of more heterosexual and antisocial activities will predict nonsymbiotic schizophrenia.

A third hypothesis, based on the expectation that symbiosis is an environmental, nongenetic factor and the earlier reports that disturbances in autonomic arousal in schizophrenic subjects also are not genetically determined (Van Dyke, Rosenthal, & Rasmussen, 1974; Zahn, 1975), is that disturbances in autonomic function will predict symbiotic schizophrenia.

Another hypothesis also reflects the belief that symbiosis is not a genetically determined phenomenon and that high genetic loading for schizophrenia will, therefore, predict nonsymbiotic schizophrenia.

The final hypothesis in this group postulates a connection

between more frequent and traumatic early separation from mothers and other caregivers and disturbed autonomic patterns (Mednick & Schulsinger, 1970). The hypothesis predicts that a history of such events will predict symbiotic schizophrenia.

The second group of hypotheses involves the subjects' responses to hospitalization and the subliminal stimulation of "Mommy and I are one." The subliminal stimulation is based on the work of Silverman and co-workers (Silverman, Lachmann, & Milich, 1982) which suggests that "better differentiated" schizophrenic patients respond to repetitive exposure to the subliminal stimulus, "Mommy and I are one," by reduction in their thought disorders.

The first hypothesis reflects the belief that separation from the symbiotic object, as occurs at the time of hospitalization, increases thought disorder; it predicts that a greater baseline thought disorder following admission to the hospital will predict symbiotic schizophrenia.

A second hypothesis, based on the report that the subliminal stimulus provides only better differentiated schizophrenic subjects with a form of symbiotic gratification (Silverman et al., 1982) is that failure in reduction of thought disorder in response to the subliminal stimulation, "Mommy and I are one," will predict symbiotic schizophrenia.

The third group of hypotheses involves the relationship between intervention efforts and the dependent variables and are based on the belief that patients with symbiotic schizophrenia are particularly vulnerable to issues of separation.

One hypothesis predicts that separation from the symbiotic parent will extend the period of initial cognitive disruption which will be less responsive to neuroleptic treatment. Improvement in the thought disorder will occur only insofar as the institution or therapist substitutes as a symbiotic object for the patient. The hypothesis is that slower resolution of psychotic symptomatology will predict symbiotic schizophrenia. Other hypotheses are: A recurrence of psychotic symptoms after a state of discharge readiness has been clinically ascertained and communicated to the subject will predict symbiotic schizophrenia; a lower prevalence of relapse upon discharge to the family of origin (as contrasted to nonfamily placement), with more restricted and structured aftercare programs, will predict symbiotic schizophrenia; and discontinuation of aftercare programs following discharge to the family of origin will predict symbiotic schizophrenia.

The hypotheses regarding the subjects' experiences with individual psychotherapy and outcome are based on the same theoretical premises. One such hypothesis is that slow engagement in psychotherapy and increased psychotic symptoms when psychotherapy is interrupted or discontinued will predict symbiotic schizophrenia in those subjects who do become engaged in psychotherapy. A second hypothesis is that with respect to independent living and employment, a worse overall outcome at two and three years after treatment will predict symbiotic schizophrenia. Other hypotheses in this group include that a greater likelihood of return to the family of origin will predict symbiotic schizophrenia, and that a longer time in the hospital will predict symbiotic schizophrenia.

A final hypothesis is the independence of all aspects of engagement in psychotherapy, discharge, aftercare, and outcome from neuroleptic utilization will predict symbiotic schizophrenia. Major inclusion criteria are that subjects have DSM-III diagnosis of Schizophrenic Disorder of two or more years duration, be hospitalized for that disorder, and be of the same socioeconomic status.

Each subject's response to interventions will be measured over a period of three years. Each subject will be assigned a psychotherapist for intensive individual psychotherapy. Each subject will be given intensive daily subliminal stimulation for two weeks, then measures of his or her thought disorder will be repeated. The patients' subsequent engagement in psychotherapy, hospital course, and outcome over the course of the next three years will be evaluated. Measures of thought disorder, signs and symptoms, and discharge readiness will be repeated throughout the three years. Engagement in and progress in psychotherapy will also be assessed periodically.

It is by incorporating variables from outside the psychodynamic discipline that the investigator may increase understanding of the importance of psychodynamic factors in the etiologies of the schizophrenias.

A LONGITUDINAL RESEARCH STUDY

Child development and the schizophrenias

In this final illustration, focus is shifted to a particular type of longitudinal research that is designed to clarify the interplay of biologic, psychologic, and social variables in the development of children at risk for the schizophrenias. The magnitude and complexity are at a different level from those of the first three examples; therefore, the description of this example will be at an even more general level than used in earlier examples.

The study would require a stable interdisciplinary team with a high level of commitment to the investigational structure. Experts from a wide range of disciplines would be required: for example, child development, psychoanalysis, child psychiatry, child neurology, neonatology, and others. Mechanisms would need to be built into the project to augment the likelihood of interdisciplinary collaboration.

This illustration borrows heavily from the relatively small number of empirical studies of child development that relate either directly or indirectly to the etiologies of the schizophrenias (Bergman & Escalona, 1949; Fish, 1977; Fish & Alpert, 1962b; Fish & Hagin, 1973; Mednick & Schulsinger, 1968; Sameroff, 1972; Sameroff & Zax, 1973, 1978; Sameroff, Seifer, & Zax, 1982; Schacter, Elmer, Ragins, Wimberly, & Lachin, 1977; Schulsinger, 1976).

There is an open-ended exploratory component to developmental studies that extend over long periods of time even though they require a model of human development and, in this instance, a model of the development of schizophrenia, as well as focused hypotheses. That is, data indicating the interaction of variables at either one or several points in the time can be useful in establishing more restricted hypotheses to be tested in smaller, cross-sectional studies.

The most general statement of the model of human development involves the interplay of biologic, psychologic, and social variables in this progressive unfolding of the child's ego integrity and sense of self. Deviation in one variable (or system of variables) influences all other variables and, in turn, is influenced by the response of those variables to the initial change. Developmental models focus particularly on the sequence of events and processes and rely often on the concept of critical periods. A large number of developmental variables have ample theoretical or empirical data to warrant their inclusion in designs investigating the etiologies of the schizophrenias. Selection of variables is complex and, in this example, we wish merely to illustrate the range of variables rather than to suggest a complete list.

In keeping with the assumptions about the schizophrenias noted earlier, we expect to find that there are multiple developmental pathways to the schizophrenias and that different domains of variables play critical roles in the different developmental pathways. Although such research emphasizes the complex interaction of etiologic variables, the development of some patients' schizophrenic syndromes may be more heavily influenced by biologic deviations, and other patients' syndromes more by psychologic or social variables.

In this example, the independent variables will be certain genetic, constitutional, family system, and phase-specific infant and childhood interactional processes within their social context (such as attachment behavior, separation-individuation, initial school experiences, pubertal experiences, and later high school graduation and marital choice experience). Certain biologic variables (e.g., DMT and platelet MAO) will be used as markers and will be assessed throughout the individual's development. The dependent variables will be the development of a Schizophrenic or Schizophreniform Disorder.

The problems associated with such developmental studies are enormous, but it has been possible in the past to design, fund, and operationalize such long-range longitudinal research. However, the few studies concerning the etiology of the schizophrenias that are currently in place commenced more recently and, we presume, search with difficulty for continued support, even though the complexity of the schizophrenic process is unlikely to yield to anything but longitudinal designs. To illustrate, the following are research questions from which specific hypotheses could be elaborated.

Questions raised by the increased prevalence of schizophrenia in the children of schizophrenic mothers bear upon selection of variables: Is the mother's capacity for appropriate attachment behavior important? Is the severity of the mother's symptomatology critical? Is the infant's temperament important? Is the nature of the mother's support systems relevant? Does the presence in the mother's life of an intimate relationship with another adult influence the infant's outcome? Are some schizophrenic mothers unable to facilitate the child's subsequent separation-individuation? What are the differences between schizophrenic women whose children do not become schizophrenic (i.e., the majority) and those whose children do become schizophrenic?

A second group of questions concerns the development of biochemical and neurophysiologic abnormalities in children at risk. When do such abnormalities develop? What is the relationship of such abnormalities to changes in the child's behavior, the mother-child interaction, the parents' marital relationship, and the life stresses affecting the family?

Another group of questions concerns the relationship of early developmental difficulties to the subsequent development of psychiatric syndromes, including schizophrenia, in children not at risk genetically for schizophrenia. (Over 90 percent of schizophrenic patients do not have a first-degree relative with the disorder.) What early developmental difficulties render a child at risk for the subsequent development of schizophrenia? Do such difficulties involve attachment behaviors, separation-individuation behaviors, the development of biochemical or neurophysiologic abnormalities, particular maternal behaviors, gross disturbances in family functioning, or deviations in other relevant systems?

A fourth group of questions involves the relationships between early developmental deviances and response to subsequent developmental challenges. For example, do infants who demonstrate anxious attachment to the mother have more problems beginning school, adapting to pubertal changes, and leaving home following graduation from school? What factors in the family system or peer relationships influence such equations? Another example involves children who demonstrate avoidant attachment with both parents. Are such children at risk for becoming "loners," remote compulsives, schizoids? Can such a child subsequently "learn" to participate in close relationships? Can a close peer or sibling relationship develop under such circumstances and, if so, does it offer the child protection from future developmental difficulties? Do difficulties in developing close relationships with others represent a risk factor for the subsequent development of Schizophrenic or Schizophreniform Disorders?

Such questions may suggest a search for simple and linear causal sequences. That is not our intent. Rather, we anticipate that complex interrelationships among processes over time will be characteristic of the etiologies of the schizophrenias.

In designing such developmental research, one must define "at high risk for schizophrenia." If one wishes to clarify the role of genetic variables, *high risk* may be defined as the degree of genetic loading within the family. If, however, one hopes to identify multiple pathways for the development of schizophrenia, it is useful to incorporate in the design several definitions of high risk. In this example, we suggest the latter option. The design calls for three groups of married women (in their initial pregnancies): schizophrenic, neurotically depressed, and those with no mental illness. Ethnicity would be controlled, and the sample would be restricted to low-income, working-class families.

The independent variables would include the genetic loading of some of the children of the schizophrenic mothers contrasted with the absence of such loading in the other two groups. Perinatal and neonatal variables would include complications of pregnancy, birth weight, problems of delivery, and neonatal status. Constitutional variables would include neurologic integration, autonomic responsivity, and temperament. Phase-specific variables to be measured would include mother-infant and father-infant attachment behavior, separation-individuation behaviors, and accomplishment of subsequent developmental challenges. Family variables would be the quality of the parental relationship prior to the child's birth and at subsequent stages of family development. The child's participation in family interactions would be assessed throughout childhood and adolescence.

Currently, a variety of techniques and instruments with which to measure this array of biologic, psychologic, and social variables are available. Although they are at various levels of sophistication, it is presumed that measures will become increasingly precise as the project evolves and that such refinements can be incorporated into the design.

Although the specific dependent variable will be the subsequent development of Schizophrenic or Schizophreniform Disorders, the design would also consider the developing social competence of the children as well as both broad and specific developmental abnormalities. Of particular relevance would be the development in childhood of behaviors pre-

sumed to be related to the subsequent development of schizophrenia such as eccentric or odd relationship patterns,
idiosyncratic cognitive styles, and affective inaccessibility.

The times of data collection include the prenatal period,
the first week of the infant's life, then at three, 12, and 36
months. Subsequent data collection would occur at the time
of starting school, the latency period, completion of puberty,
high school graduation, the time of marital choice, and after
the first year of marriage.

These brief, oversimplified examples are not, of course,
formal research designs; rather, they are meant to suggest
how both current clinical understanding of the schizophrenias and cross-domain research can be useful in increasing
understanding of the etiologies of the schizophrenias.

5

IMPLICATIONS FOR TREATMENT
AND TRAINING

Although this report is concerned primarily with the need for cross-domain research in order to further our understanding of the schizophrenias, we wish to note briefly the implications of this emphasis for both clinicians and those responsible for training psychiatrists and other mental health professionals. Clinicians responsible for the treatment of patients with Schizophrenic Disorders need to understand the complexity inherent in the application of this diagnosis, in particular, the variability of causal factors, future courses, and outcomes. If this complexity is recognized, it has major implications for how one approaches clinical situations involving patients with Schizophrenic Disorders. The following observations describe four such implications:

1) *Schizophrenic patients need extensive evaluations.* When an evaluation is limited to the issue of whether a patient fulfills criteria for DSM-III diagnosis of Schizophrenic Disorder, it is not possible to say very much about the cause, treatment, and future course of a specific patient. In this report we have tried to convey that the clinician must consider a wide range of variables including those from the domains of biology, psychology, and sociology.

2) *The treatment of patients with Schizophrenic Disorders should be individualized.* Throughout this report we have referred to "the schizophrenias" in order to emphasize the heterogeneity of these disorders. One patient may need help separating from an enmeshed family, whereas another may need spe-

cialized help in developing an increased ability to focus attention, and a third may need long-term intensive psychotherapy. Therefore, no single treatment program can be expected to be ideal under all circumstances. Outpatient psychotherapists and hospital treatment programs alike need to be flexible in their orientation or, if not, make appropriate referrals to other individuals or programs that are better suited to the treatment needs of a particular patient.

3) *The treatment of patients with Schizophrenic Disorders should be multimodal.* The range of deficits in such patients will vary considerably, and only rarely will they be confined to one area. The multiplicity of such deficits requires treatment plans that address each of the problems. This may mean a multidisciplinary team approach utilizing professionals with different skills. The importance of the coordination of such clinical efforts is obvious.

4) *Clinicians must be cautious in offering patients or their families explanations of the patients' Schizophrenic Disorders.* It is difficult for a psychiatrist or other mental health professional to resist the demand from patients' families (or the general public) for simple answers, but overly simple explanations do not reflect the biopsychosocial reality of the schizophrenias. In clinical experience an authoritative approach is helpful with some patients or their families in order to diminish anxiety, but the approach should stop short of a too simple explanation of the cause of the Schizophrenic Disorder. These issues are very complex, and our knowledge so limited.

These implications have in common the need to recognize the narrowness of current knowledge and the need to use significant clinical judgment. There is no one "correct" approach to the treatment of patients who are experiencing various forms of Schizophrenic Disorders. Indeed, the clinician needs to individualize treatment approaches, including the possibility of innovative and creative treatment parameters. From such experience the clinician's observations about Schizophrenic Disorders will continue to be the most profitable base for developing better models about the nature of the schizophrenias.

The central thesis of this report has implications also for those whose primary involvement is training psychiatrists and other professionals. What has been said about the complexity of the schizophrenias underscores the importance of teaching a way of thinking about the etiologies of these disorders that reflects the role of multiple domains and many variables. Therefore, students need to be introduced to the complexity of these syndromes without either oversimplification or focus on a single domain. Present gaps in our knowledge need to be presented with equal clarity. Competing theoretical models of the schizophrenias should be presented; they stimulate thought and study.

The schizophrenias often have an unclear onset and a long course, which makes it helpful to the trainee to have a clear understanding of the basic concepts of child and adolescent development as well as clinical experience with intensive, long-term treatment modalities of individuals with these syndromes by which to observe the interactions between life events, relationships, and fluctuations in symptoms.

Many training programs are located in institutions or departments in which there is a major emphasis upon biology, psychology, or sociology. Trainees in such institutions or departments, in particular, need to be introduced to a broadly based understanding of the biopsychosocial factors involved in the etiologies of the schizophrenias. In a parallel manner, trainees need to become comfortable with using a wide variety of treatment modalities. Biologic, psychologic, and social treatments are each useful and necessary in the treatment of many patients with Schizophrenic Disorders. Reliance on a single treatment modality is usually inadequate.

Finally, it should be emphasized to trainees that there is no incompatibility between the development of clinical skills and the ability to conceptualize research hypotheses. The curiosity of clinicians dealing with patients with such disor-

ders remains a major pathway to important research hypotheses. In a comparable way, the acquisition of sophisticated
clinical skills is an invaluable asset in planning and accom-
plishing research projects.

6
CONCLUSION

A review of the research literature on the etiologies of the schizophrenias suggests that most of such research is based on the strategies and techniques developed for individual disciplines within a single domain. These have been fruitful, and much has been learned about the biology, psychology, and sociology of these syndromes. From an etiologic perspective there is increasing recognition that the schizophrenias are heterogeneous. It is not likely, therefore, that a single cause that is both necessary and sufficient will be found. Rather, as in hypertension and other chronic medical illnesses, there are risk factors that, in certain constellations, can produce various forms of the syndrome.

From the perspective of the treatment of the schizophrenias, both the heterogeneity of the disorders and clinical experience suggest that the search for a "magic bullet" with which to "cure" all forms of the syndrome is unlikely to be productive. Rather, selected treatments from each domain will be required in a blend that may be unique to each form of the syndrome and, perhaps, even unique to each patient.

Because of the accumulation of evidence that the schizophrenias result from complex interactions of biologic, psychologic, and social variables, this report recommends an increased emphasis on cross-domain research. In making this recommendation we do not minimize the importance of continued single-discipline or cross-discipline research within a single domain. Rather, we can anticipate that new and powerful etiologic variables in each domain will be brought to

light, and study of the interaction between such variables and
variables from other domains will advance understanding of
the schizophrenias.

Cross-domain research necessarily involves teams of investigators because few, if any, individuals are competent to
conduct rigorous research in more than one domain. The
report suggests a few of the difficulties involved in main-
taining productive cross-domain research teams. Nonethe-
less, much can be gained from serious efforts in this direction.
Without such cooperative efforts we can anticipate increasing
refinement in each domain without, however, sufficient integration across domains.

In addition to the pragmatic difficulties involved in cross-
domain research, the report addresses other problems that
a biopsychosocial orientation to the etiologies of the schizophrenias highlights. There is a need for the continued development of multiple and complex theoretical models of the
schizophrenias and a need to develop statistical techniques
that assess the interactive properties of variables from all
domains adequately. Clinicians and investigators involved
with severe and often chronic disorders other than schizophrenia face many of the same problems. Untangling the
complex interactions of biologic, psychologic, and social variables involved in predisposing to, precipitating, and sustaining disease continues to challenge all concerned with the
alleviation of human suffering.

REFERENCES

Ainsworth, M. D. S. (1964). Patterns of attachment behavior shown by the infant in interaction with his mother. *Merrill-Palmer Quarterly, 10,* 51-58.

Ainsworth, M. D. S. (1970). The development of infant-mother attachment. In B. M. Caldwell & P. Ricciuti (Eds.), *Review of Child Development, Vol. 2.* New York: Russell Sage Foundation.

Anthony, E. J. (1974). The syndrome of the psychologically vulnerable child. In E. J. Anthony & C. Koupernik (Eds.), *The Child in His Family: Children at Psychiatric Risk, Vol. 3.* New York: John Wiley & Sons, 3-10.

Arieti, S. (1974). *Interpretation of Schizophrenia,* 2nd Ed. New York: Basic Books.

Asarnow, R. F., & MacCrimmon, D. J. (1978). Residual performance deficit in clinically remitted schizophrenics. A marker of schizophrenia? *Journal of Abnormal Psychology, 87,* 597-608.

Asarnow, R. F., & MacCrimmon, D. J. (1981). Span of apprehension deficits during the postpsychotic stages of schizophrenia. *Archives of General Psychiatry, 38,* 1006-1011.

Asarnow, R. F., Steffy, R. A., MacCrimmon, D. J., & Cleghorn, J. M. (1977). An attentional assessment of foster children at risk for schizophrenia. *Journal of Abnormal Psychology, 86,* 267-275.

Bakan, P. (1968). *Disease, Pain, and Sacrifice. Toward a Psychology of Suffering.* Chicago: University of Chicago Press.

Bateson, G., Jackson, D., Haley, J., & Weakland, J. (1956). Toward a theory of schizophrenia. *Behavioral Science, 1,* 241-264.

Bauman, E., & Murray, D. J. (1968). Recognition versus recall in schizophrenia. *Canadian Journal of Psychology, 22,* 18-25.

Bellak, L., & Loeb, L. (Eds.) (1969). *The Schizophrenic Syndrome.* New York: Grune & Stratton.

Bergman, P., & Escalona, S. K. (1949). Unusual sensitivities in very young children. In *The Psychoanalytic Study of the Child, Vol. 3(4),* 333-352.

Birch, H. G., & Hertzig, M. (1967). Etiology of schizophrenia: An overview of the relation of development to atypical behavior. In J. Romano (Ed.), *The Origins of Schizophrenia.* The Hague, Netherlands: Excerpta Medica Foundation.

Bleuler, E. (1950). *Dementia Praecox or the Group of Schizophrenias.* New York: International Universities Press.

Bleuler, M. (1941). *Krankheitsverlauf, Personlichkeith, und Verwandtschaft*

Schizophrener und Ihre Gegenseitigen Beziehungen. Leipzig, East Ger-
many: Thieme.

Bloch, D. (1979, Spring). Donald Bloch at three major meetings: An interview.
Ackerman Institute for Family Therapy Newsletter.

Bowen, M. (1960). A family concept of schizophrenia. In D. D. Jackson (Ed.),
The Etiology of Schizophrenia. New York: Basic Books. 346-372.

Bowers, M. B., Jr. (1974). *Retreat from Sanity: The Structure of Emerging
Psychosis.* New York: Human Sciences Press.

Bowlby, J. (1969). *Attachment and Loss, Vol. 1.* New York: Basic Books.

Bridger, W. H. (1961). Sensory habituation and discrimination in the human
neonate. *American Journal of Psychiatry, 117,* 991-996.

Brown, G. W., & Birley, J. L. T. (1968). Crises and life changes and the onset
of schizophrenia. *Journal of Health & Social Behavior, 9*(3), 203-214.

Brown, G. W., Birley, J. L. T., & Wing, J. K. (1972). Influence of family on
the course of schizophrenic disorders: A replication. *British Journal of
Psychiatry, 121,* 241-258.

Buchsbaum, M., & Haier, R. (1978). Biological homogeneity, symptom heterogeneity, and the diagnosis of schizophrenia. *Schizophrenia Bulletin,
4,* 373-375.

Cancro, R. (1980). Overview of schizophrenia. In H. I. Kaplan, A. M. Freedman, & B. J. Sadock (Eds.), *Comprehensive Textbook of Psychiatry, III.*
Baltimore: Williams & Wilkins.

Carpenter, W. T., Fink, E. B., Narasimhachari, N., & Himwich, H. E. (1975).
A test of the transmethylation hypothesis in acute schizophrenic patients.
American Journal of Psychiatry, 132, 1067-1071.

Cassell, J. (1976). The contribution of the social environment to host resistance.
American Journal of Epidemiology, 104(2), 107-123.

Caudill, W. (1958). Effects of social and cultural systems in reaction to stress.
Social Science Research Council, Pamphlet #14, New York.

Cheek, F. E. (1965). The father of the schizophrenic. *Archives of General
Psychiatry, 13,* 336-345.

Clark, R. E. (1948). The relationship of schizophrenia to occupational income
and occupational prestige. *American Sociological Review, 13,* 325-330.

Clausen, J. A., & Kohn, M. L. (1959). Relation of schizophrenia to the structure
of a small city. In B. Pasamanick (Ed.), *Epidemiology of Mental Disorder.*
Washington, DC: American Association for the Advancement of Science,
69.

Doane, J. A., West, K. L., Goldstein, M. J., Rodnick, E. H., & Jones, J. E.
(1981). Parental communication deviance and affective style: Predictors

of subsequent schizophrenia spectrum disorders in vulnerable adolescents. *Archives of General Psychiatry, 38,* 679-685.

Dubos, R. (1965). *Man Adapting.* New Haven: Yale University Press.

Elder, G. H. (1979). Historical change in life patterns and personality. In P. B. Baltes & L. G. Brim, Jr. (Eds.), *Life Span Development and Behavior, Vol. 2.* New York: Academic Press.

Engel, G. L. (1977). The need for a new medical model: A challenge for biomedicine. *Science, 196*(4286), 129-136.

Engel, G. L. (1979). The biopsychosocial model. Resolving the conflict between medicine and psychiatry. *Resident and Staff Physician, 25*(7), 72.

Falloon, I. R. H., & Lieberman, R. P. (1983). Behavioral family intervention in the management of chronic schizophrenics. In W. R. McFarlane (Ed.), *Family Therapy in Schizophrenia.* New York: Guilford Press.

Faris, R. E. L., & Dunham, H. W. (1939). *Mental Disorders in Urban Areas.* Chicago: University of Chicago Press.

Fischer, M. (1974). Genetic and environmental factors in schizophrenia. *Acta Psychiatrica Scandinavica, 238* (Suppl.), 1-158.

Fish, B. (1977). Neurobiologic antecedents of schizophrenia in children. *Archives of General Psychiatry, 34,* 1297-1313.

Fish, B., & Alpert, M. S. (1962a). Abnormal states of consciousness and muscle tone in infants born to schizophrenic mothers. *American Journal of Psychiatry, 119,* 439-445.

Fish, B., & Alpert, M. (1962b). Patterns of neurological development in infants born to schizophrenic mothers. In J. Wortis (Ed.), *Recent Advances in Biological Psychiatry, Vol. 4.* New York: Plenum Press.

Fish, B., & Hagin, R. (1973). Visual-motor disorders in infants at risk for schizophrenia. *Archives of General Psychiatry, 28,* 900-904.

Fish, B., Shapiro, T., Halpern, F., & Wile, R. (1965). The prediction of schizophrenia in infancy: III. A ten-year follow-up report of neurological and psychological development. *American Journal of Psychiatry, 121,* 768-775.

Forrester, J. W. (1969). *Urban Dynamics.* Boston: M. I. T. Press.

Freud, S. (1953). *Three Essays on the Theory of Sexuality (1905) S.E., Vol. 7.* London: Hogarth Press.

Freud, S. (1954). *The Origins of Psychoanalysis: Letters to Wilhelm Fliess, Drafts and Notes: 1887-1902.* M. Bonaparte, A. Freud, & E. Kris (Eds.), New York: Basic Books.

Freud, S. (1955). *Studies in Hysteria (1893-95) S.E. Vol. 2.* London: Hogarth Press.

Fromm-Reichmann, F. (1948). Notes on the development of treatment of schizophrenia by psychoanalytic psychotherapy. *Psychiatry, 11,* 263-273.

Garmezy, N., & Streitman, S. (1974). Children at risk: The search for the antecedents of schizophrenia. Part I. Conceptual models and research methods. *Schizophrenia Bulletin, 8,* 14-90.

Goldhamer, H., & Marshall, A. W. (1953). *Psychosis and Civilization.* Salem, NH: Arno.

Gossett, J. T., Meeks, J. E., Barnhart, F. D., & Phillips, V. A. (1976). Follow-up of adolescents treated in a psychiatric hospital: Onset of Symptomatology Scale. *Adolescence, 2,* 195-211.

Gottesman, I. I., & Shields, J. (1976). A critical review of recent adoption, twin, and family studies of schizophrenia: Behavioral genetics perspectives. *Schizophrenia Bulletin, 2,* 360-401.

Heston, L. L. (1966). Psychiatric disorders in foster home reared children of schizophrenic mothers. *British Journal of Psychiatry, 112,* 819-825.

Hollingshead, A. B., & Redlich, F. C. (1958). *Social Class and Mental Illness: A Community Study.* New York: John Wiley & Son, Inc., 232.

Holmes, T. H., & Rahe, R. H. (1967). The social readjustment rating scale. *Journal of Psychosomatic Research, 11,* 213-218.

Holzman, P. S., Proctor, L. R., & Hughes, D. S. (1973). Eyetracking patterns in schizophrenia. *Science, 181,* 179-181.

Holzman, P. S., Proctor, L. R., Levy, D. L., Yasillo, N. J., Meltzer, H. Y., & Hurt, S. W. (1974). Eyetracking dysfunctions in schizophrenic patients and their relatives. *Archives of General Psychiatry, 31,* 143-151.

Jacobs, S., & Myers, J. (1976). Recent life events and acute schizophrenic psychosis: A controlled study. *Journal of Nervous and Mental Disease, 162*(2), 75-87.

Jung, C. G. (1936). *The Psychology of Dementia Praecox, Monograph 3.* New York: Nervous and Mental Disease Publishing Company.

Kafka, J. S. (1971). Ambiguity for individuation: A critique and reformulation of double-bind theory. *Archives of General Psychiatry, 25,* 232-237.

Kallman, F. G. (1938). *The Genetics of Schizophrenia.* Locust Valley, NY: Augustin.

Kallman, F. J. (1946). The genetic theory of schizophrenia: An analysis of 691 schizophrenic twin index families. *American Journal of Psychiatry, 103,* 309-322.

Kandel, E. R. (1979, Nov. 6). Psychotherapy and the single synapse. *New England Journal of Medicine,* 1028-1037

Kaplan, A. (1976). *Human Behavior Genetics.* Springfield, IL: Charles C Thomas.

Karlsson, J. L. (1970). Genetic association of giftedness and creativity with schizophrenia. *Herediatas, 66,* 177.

Karlsson, J. L. (1973). An Icelandic family study of schizophrenia. *British Journal of Psychiatry, 123,* 549-554.

Kety, S. S., Rosenthal, D., Wender, P. H., & Schulsinger, F. (1968). The types and prevalence of mental illness in the biological and adoptive families of adopted schizophrenics. In D. Rosenthal, & S. Kety (Eds.), *The Transmission of Schizophrenia.* Oxford, England: Pergamon Press.

Kety, S. S., Rosenthal, D., Wender, P. H., Schulsinger, F., & Jacobson, B. (1975). Mental illness in the biological and adoptive families of adopted individuals who have been schizophrenic: A preliminary report based on psychiatric interviews. In R. F. Fieve, D. Rosenthal, & H. Brill (Eds.), *Genetic Research in Psychiatry.* Baltimore: Johns Hopkins University Press.

Klaus, M. H., Jerauld, R., Kreger, N. C., McAlpine, W., Steffa, M., & Kennell, J. H. (1972). Maternal attachment: Importance of first post-partum days. *New England Journal of Medicine, 286,* 460-463.

Klerman, G. L. (1978). The evolution of a scientific nosology. In J. C. Shershaw (Ed.), *Schizophrenia, Science, and Practice.* Cambridge, MA: Harvard University Press, 99-122.

Koh, D. S., & Kayton, L. (1974). Memorization of "unrelated" word strings by young nonpsychotic schizophrenics. *Journal of Abnormal Psychology, 83,* 14-22.

Kraepelin, E. (1918). *Dementia Praecox.* London: E. and S. Livingstone.

Kraepelin, E. (1921). *Manic-depressive Insanity and Paranoia.* Edinburgh, England: E. and S. Livingstone.

Kraepelin, E. (1962). *One Hundred Years of Psychiatry.* New York: Citadel Press.

Kraepelin, E. (1968). *Lectures on Clinical Psychiatry.* New York: Hafner Press.

Kringlen, E. (1967). *Heredity and Environment in the Functional Psychoses: An Epidemiological-Clinical Twin Study.* London: Heinermann.

Landau, S. G., Buchsbaum, M. S., Carpenter, W., Strauss, J., & Sacks, M. (1975). Schizophrenia and stimulus intensity control. *Archives of General Psychiatry, 32,* 1239-1254.

Langer, T. S., & Michael, S. T. (1963). *Life Stress and Mental Health.* New York: Free Press of Glencoe.

Leff, J. P. (1976). Schizophrenia and sensitivity to the family environment. *Schizophrenia Bulletin, 2,* 566-574.

Leff, J. P., Berkowitz, R., Kuipers, L. (1983). Intervention in families of schizo-phrenics and its effects on relapse rate. In W. R. McFarlane (Ed.), *Family Therapy in Schizophrenia.* New York: Guilford Press.

Leff, J. P., & Vaughn, C. (1980). The interaction of life events and relatives' expressed emotion in schizophrenia and depressive neurosis. *British Journal of Psychiatry, 136,* 146-153.

Lewis, J. M., Beavers, W. R., Gossett, J. T., & Phillips, V. A. (1976). *No Single Thread: Psychological Health in Family Systems.* New York: Brunner/Mazel.

Lidz, T., Blatt, S., & Cook, B. (1981). Critique of the Danish American studies of the adopted-away offspring of schizophrenic parents. *American Journal of Psychiatry, 138*(8), 1063-1068.

Lidz, T., Cornelison, A., Fleck, S., & Terry, D. (1957). The intrafamilial environment of schizophrenic patients II: Marital schism and marital skew. *American Journal of Psychiatry, 114,* 241-248.

Lidz, T., Cornelison, A., Terry, D., & Fleck, S. (1958). Intrafamilial environment of the schizophrenic patient: VI. The transmission of irrationality. *Archives of Neurology and Psychiatry, 79,* 305-316.

Lidz, R. W., & Lidz, T. (1949). The family environment of schizophrenic patients. *American Journal of Psychiatry, 106,* 332-345.

Lipton, E. L., Steinschneider, A., & Richmond, J. B. (1965). The autonomic nervous system in early life. *New England Journal of Medicine, 273,* 147-153.

MacCrimmon, D. J., Cleghorn, J. M., Asarnow, R. F., & Steffy, R. A. (1980). Children at risk for schizophrenia: Clinical and attentional characteristics. *Archives of General Psychiatry, 37,* 671-674.

Mahler, M. S., Pine, F., & Bergman, A. (1975). *Psychological Birth of the Human Infant.* New York: Basic Books.

Main, M., & Weston, D. R. (1982). Avoidance of the attachment figure in infancy: Descriptions and interpretations. In C. M. Parkes, & J. Stevenson-Hinde (Eds.), *The Place of Attachment in Human Behavior.* New York: Basic Books.

Malzberg, B., & Less, E. S. (1956). *Migration and Mental Disease.* New York: Social Science Research Council.

Marcus, J. (1973). Schizophrenic offspring—infant studies. PL 480, No. 06-278-2. Hebrew University Medical School. Jerusalem, Israel. Cited in L. Mosher, & J. Gunderson, with S. Buchsbaum. Special Report: Schizophrenia, 1972. *Schizophrenia Bulletin,* Winter, 7, p. 27.

McReynolds, P. (1960). Anxiety, perception, and schizophrenia. In D. Jackson (Ed.), *The Etiology of Schizophrenia.* New York: Basic Books.

Mednick, S. A. (1958). A learning theory approach to research in schizophrenia. *Psychological Bulletin, 55,* 316-327.

Mednick, S. A., & Schulsinger, F. (1968). Some premorbid characteristics related to breakdown in children with schizophrenic mothers. In D. Rosenthal, & S. S. Kety (Eds.), *The Transmission of Schizophrenia*. Oxford, England: Pergamon Press.

Mednick, S. A., & Schulsinger, F. (1970). Factors related to breakdown in children at high risk for schizophrenia. In M. Roff, & D. F. Ricks (Eds.), *Life History Research in Psychopathology, Vol. 1*. Minneapolis: University of Minnesota Press.

Meyer, A. (1957). *Psychobiology: A Science of Man*. Springfield, IL: Charles C Thomas.

Moss, G. E. (1973). *Illness, Immunity, and Social Interaction: The Dynamics of Biosocial Resonation*. New York: John Wiley and Sons.

Mourer, S. A. (1973). A prediction of patterns of schizophrenic error resulting from semantic generalization. *Journal of Abnormal Psychology, 81*, 250-254.

Murphy, H. B. M. (1967). Sociocultural factors in schizophrenia: A compromise theory. In J. Zubin, & F. Freyhan (Eds.), *Social Psychiatry*. New York: Grune & Stratton, 74-92.

Murray, R. M., Oon, M. C. H., Rodnight, R., Birley, J. L. T., & Smith, A. (1979). Increased excretion of dimethyltryptamine and certain features of psychosis. *Archives of General Psychiatry, 36*, 644-649.

Nachmani, G., & Cohen, B. D. (1969). Recall and recognition-free learning in schizophrenics. *Journal of Abnormal Psychology, 74*, 511-516.

Neuchterlein, K. H. (1977). Reaction time and attention in schizophrenia: A critical evaluation of the data and theories. *Schizophrenia Bulletin, 3*(3), 373-428.

Odegaard, O. (1932). Emigration and insanity. *Acta Psychiatrica et Neurologic Scandinavica, 4*, (Suppl.).

Odegaard, O. (1972). The multifactorial theory of inheritance in predisposition to schizophrenia. In A. R. Kaplan (Ed.), *Genetic Factors in "Schizophrenia."* Springfield, IL: Charles C Thomas.

Opler, M. K., & Singer, J. (1956). Ethnic differences in behavior and psychopathology: Italians and Irish. *International Journal of Social Psychiatry, 2*, 11.

Pasamanick, B., & Knobloch, H. (1961). Epidemiological studies on the complications of pregnancy and the birth process. In G. Kaplan (Ed.), *Prevention of Mental Disorders in Children*. New York: Basic Books.

Paykel, E. S., Prusoff, B. A., & Myers, J. K. (1975). Suicide attempts and recent life events. *Archives of General Psychiatry, 32*, 327-333.

Payne, R. W. (1973). Cognitive abnormalities. In H. J. Eysenck (Ed.), *Handbook of Abnormal Psychology (2nd ed.)* London: Pitman Medical Press.

Pollin, W., Allen, M. G., Hoffer, A., Stabenau, J. R., & Hrubec, Z. (1969). Psychopathology in 15,909 pairs of veteran twins. *American Journal of Psychiatry, 126,* 597-610.

Rahe, R. H., Mahan, J. L., Arthur, R. J., Gunderson, E. K. E. (1970). The epidemiology of illness in Naval environments: I: Illness types, distribution, severity, and relationship to life change. *Military Medicine, 135*(6), 443-452.

Raven, P. H., Berlin, B., & Breedlove, D. E. (1971). The origins of taxonomy. *Science, 174,* 1210-1213.

Reiss, D. (1975). Families and the etiology of schizophrenia. *Schizophrenia Bulletin, 14,* 9-11.

Reiss, D., & Wyatt, R. (1975). Family and biologic variables in the same etiologic studies of schizophrenia. *Schizophrenia Bulletin, 14,* 64-81.

Ricks, D., & Nameche, G. (1966). Symbiosis, sacrifice, and schizophrenia. *Mental Hygiene, 50,* 541-544.

Rodnight, R., Murray, R. M., Oon, M. C. H., Brockington, I. F., Nicholls, P., & Birley, J. L. T. (1976). Urinary dimethyltryptamine and psychiatric symptomatology and classification. *Psychological Medicine, 6,* 649-657.

Rogler, L. H., & Hollingshead, A. B. (1965). *Trapped: Families and Schizophrenia.* New York: John Wiley & Sons.

Rosenthal, D., Wender, P. H., Kety, S. S., Schulsinger, F., Weiner, J., & Ostergard, L. (1968). Schizophrenics' offspring reared in adoptive homes. In D. Rosenthal, & S. S. Kety (Eds.), *The Transmission of Schizophrenia.* Oxford, England: Pergamon Press.

Rüdin, E. (1916). *Zur Vererbung und Neuentehung der Dementia Praecox.* Berlin: Springer.

Sameroff, A. (1972). Early influences on development. *Merrill-Palmer Quarterly of Behavior and Development, 21,* 267-294.

Sameroff, A. J., Seifer, R., & Zax, M. (1982). Early development of children at risk for emotional disorder. *Monographs of the Society for Research in Child Development, 47*(7), 14-15.

Sameroff, A. J., & Zax, M. (1973). Schizotaxia revisited: Model issues in the etiology of schizophrenia. *American Journal of Orthopsychiatry, 42,* 744-754.

Sameroff, A. J., & Zax, M. (1978). In search of schizophrenia: Young offspring of schizophrenic women. In L. C. Wynne, R. L. Cromwell, & S. Mathysse (Eds.), *The Nature of Schizophrenia: New Approaches to Research and*

Treatment. New York: John Wiley & Sons.

Sander, L. W. S. (1962). Issues of early mother-child interaction. *Journal of the American Academy of Child Psychiatry, 1,* 141-166.

Satorious, N., Jablensky, A., & Shapiro, R. (1977). Two year follow-up of the patients included in the WHO international pilot study of schizophrenia. *Psychological Medicine, 7,* 529-541.

Schacter, J., Elmer, E., Ragins, N., Wimberly, F., & Lachin, J. M. (1977). Assessment of mother-infant interaction: Schizophrenic and nonschizophrenic mothers. *Merrill-Palmer Quarterly of Behavior and Development, 23*(3), 193-206.

Scheflen, R. E. (1981). *Levels of Schizophrenia.* New York: Brunner/Mazel.

Schulsinger, H. (1976). A 10-year follow-up of children with schizophrenic mothers. *Acta Psychiatrica Scandanavica, 63,* 371-386.

Schultz, B. (1932). Zur erpathologie der schizophrenia. *Z. Gersmte Neurol. Psychiatr., 143,* 175.

Searles, H. F. (1965). *Collected Papers on Schizophrenia and Related Subjects.* New York: International Universities Press.

Selye, H. (1956). *The Stress of Life.* New York: McGraw-Hill.

Shagass, C., Amadeo, M., & Overton, D. S. (1974). Eyetracking performance in psychiatric patients. *Biological Psychiatry, 9,* 245-260.

Shagass, C., Roemer, R. A., & Amadeo, M. (1976). Eyetracking performance and engagement of attention. *Archives of General Psychiatry, 33,* 121-125.

Shakow, D. (1963). Psychological deficit in schizophrenia. *Behavioral Science, 8,* 275-305.

Silverman, L. H., Lachmann, F. M., & Milich, R. H. (1982). *The Search for Oneness.* New York: International Universities Press.

Slater, E., & Shields, J. (1953). *Psychotic and Neurotic Illnesses in Twins.* London: Her Majesty's Stationery Office.

Spitz, R. A. (1945). Hospitalism: An inquiry into the genesis of the psychiatric conditions in early childhood. In A. Freud, H. Hartmann, & E. Kris (Eds.), *The Psychoanalytic Study of the Child, Vol. I.* New York: International Universities Press, 53-74.

Steinglass, P. (1978). The conceptualization of marriage from a systems theory perspective. In T. J. Paolino, Jr., & B. S. McCrady (Eds.), *Marriage and Marital Therapy.* New York: Brunner/Mazel, 298-367.

Stierlin, H. (1975). Some therapeutic implications of a transactional theory of schizophrenia. In J. Gunderson, & L. Mosher (Eds.), *Psychotherapy of Schizophrenia.* New York: Jason Aronson.

Stott, D. H., & Latchford, P. A. (1978). Prenatal antecedents of child health, development, and behavior: An epidemiological report of incidence and association. *Journal of the American Academy of Child Psychiatry, 15,* 161-191.

Strauss, J., Loevsky, L., Glazer, W., & Leaf, P. (in press). Organizing the complexities of schizophrenia. *Journal of Nervous and Mental Disease.*

Sullivan, H. S. (1953). *Conceptions of Modern Psychiatry.* New York: W. W. Norton.

Thomas, A., Birch, H. G., Chess, S., Hertzig, M. E., & Korn, S. (1965). *Behavioral Individuality in Early Childhood.* New York: New York University Press.

Thomas, A., & Chess, S. (1977). *Temperament and Development.* New York: Brunner/Mazel.

Tienari, P. (1968). Schizophrenia in monozygotic male twins. In D. Rosenthal, & S. S. Kety (Eds.), *The Transmission of Schizophrenia.* London: Pergamon Press, 27-36.

Tsuang, M. T., Crowe, R. R., Winokur, G., & Clancy, J. (1978). Relatives of schizophrenics, manics, depressives, and controls: An interview study of 1,331 first-degree relatives. In L. C. Wynne, R. L. Cromwell, & S. Matthysse (Eds.), *The Nature of Schizophrenia: New Approaches to Research and Treatment.* New York: John Wiley & Sons.

Vaillant, G. E. (1977). *Adaptation to Life.* Boston: Little, Brown & Co.

Van Dyke, J. L., Rosenthal, D., & Rasmussen, P. V. (1974). Electrodermal functioning in adopted-away offspring of schizophrenics. *Journal of Psychiatric Research, 10,* 199-215.

Vaughn, C. E., & Leff, J. P. (1976). The measurement of expressed emotion in the families of psychiatric patients. *British Journal of Social and Clinical Psychology, 15* (part 2), 157-165.

Waxler, N. E. (1979). Is outcome for schizophrenia better in nonindustrial societies? The case of Sri Lanka. *The Journal of Nervous and Mental Disease, 167*(3), 144-158.

Weakland, J. H. (1977). Family somatics—A neglected edge. *Family Process, 16*(3), 263-272.

Weiner, H. (1977). *Psychobiology and Human Disease.* New York: Elsevier.

Weiner, H. (1980). Schizophrenia: Etiology. In H. I. Kaplan, A. M. Freedman, & B. J. Sadock (Eds.), *Comprehensive Textbook of Psychiatry, III.* Baltimore: Williams & Wilkins.

Wender, P. H., Rosenthal, D., & Kety, S. S. (1968). A psychiatric assessment of the adoptive parents of schizophrenics. In D. Rosenthal, & S. S. Kety (Eds.), *The Transmission of Schizophrenia*. London: Pergamon Press.

Wender, P. H., Rosenthal, D., Kety, S. S., Schulsinger, F., & Weiner, J. (1973). Social class and psychopathology in adoptees: A natural experimental method for separating the roles of genetic and experiential factors. *Archives of General Psychiatry, 28,* 318-325.

Wender, P. H., Rosenthal, D., Kety, S. S., Schulsinger, F., & Weiner, J. (1974). Crossfostering: A research strategy for clarifying the role of genetic and experiential factors in the etiology of schizophrenia. *Archives of General Psychiatry, 30,* 121-128.

Wilson, E. O. (1977). Biology and the social sciences. *Daedalus, 2,* 127-140.

Wohlberg, C. W., & Kornetsky, C. (1973). Sustained attention in remitted schizophrenics. *Archives of General Psychiatry, 28,* 533-537.

Wynne, L. C., & Singer, M. T. (1963a). Thought disorder and family relations of schizophrenics: I. A research study. *Archives of General Psychiatry, 9,* 191-198.

Wynne, L. C., & Singer, M. T. (1963b). Thought disorder and family relations in schizophrenics: II. A classification of forms of thinking. *Archives of General Psychiatry, 9,* 199-206.

Wynne, L. C., Singer, M. T., Bartko, J. J., & Toohey, M. L. (1975). Schizophrenics and their families: Recent research on parental communication. In J. M. Tanner (Ed.), *Psychiatric Research: The Widening Perspective*. New York: International Universities Press.

Zahn, T. P. (1975). Psychophysiological concomitants of task performance in schizophrenia. In M. L. Kietzman, S. Sutton, & J. Zubin (Eds.), *Experimental Approaches to Pschopathology*. New York: Academic Press, Inc.

INDEX

Adolescence, 27, 52
Adoptive studies, 16, 17, 18
Ainsworth, M. D. S., 25
Allen, M. G., 16
Alpert, M. S., 21, 26, 56
Amadeo, M., 19
Anthony, E. J., 15
Arieti, S., 15, 52
Arthur, R. J., 31
Asarnow, R. F., 19
Asarnow, R. F., et al. (1977), 19
Attachment, 25-26, 58, 59
Attention deficits, 19
Autonomic arousal, disorders of, 27, 53-54

Bakan, P., 7
Barnhart, F. D., 50
Bartko, J. J., 29
Bateson, G., et al., 28
Bauman, E., 20
Beavers, W. R., 7
Bellak, L., 15
Bergman, A., 26
Bergman, P., 26, 56
Berkowitz, R., 30
Berlin, B., 6
Biochemical studies, 21-24
Birch, H. G., 25, 26
Birley, J. L. T., 29, 31, 46
Blatt, S., 17
Bleuler, E., 13, 19
Bleuler, M., 7, 15
Bloch, D., 4
Bonding, 25-26
Bowen, M., 28, 52
Bowers, M. B., Jr., 10
Bowlby, J., 25-26
Breedlove, D. E., 6
Bridger, W. H., 26
Brockington, I. F., 46
Brown, G. W., 29, 31
Buchsbaum, M., 7

Camberwell Interview, 29
Cancro, R., 15
Carpenter, W. T., et al., 19, 46
Cassell, J., 7
Caudill, W., 7

Causality, 4. *See also* Etiology
    complex models of, 6-9
    single/multiple domain models, 5-6
Central dopamine receptor
        dysfunction, 22
Cheek, F. E., 52
Chess, S., 26
Child development, and
        schizophrenias, 24-27, 56-61
Clancy, J., 15
Clark, R. E., 31
Clausen, J. A., 32
Cleghorn, J. M., 19
Cognitive deficits, 18, 20
Cohen, B. D., 20
Communication
    deviant, 18, 50-51
    "double-binding," 28-29, 33
    parental, 28-29, 38-39, 49, 50-51
Concretism, 20
Consanguinity studies, 15, 17
Continuous Performance Test, 19
Cook, B., 17
Cornelison, A., 28
Crisis, model of causality in, 8-9
Critical periods, 57
Crowe, R. R., 15
Cultural variables, 30-31, 33

Delusions, 10
Developmental studies, 21, 24-30, 56-61
Diagnosis, 23, 40
Dimethyltryptamine (DMT), 46
Disease
    biopsychosocial model of, 8, 30
    complex model of, 7-8, 9
Disease process, 13
Doane, J. A., et al., 38
Domains, research, 4
Dopamine hypothesis, 22
Double-bind theory, 28-29, 33
Dubos, R., 7
Dunham, H. W., 31

Elder, G. H., 42
Elmer, E., 56
Engel, G. L., 8

81